THE

JEWS OF BARNOW

STORIES

BY

KARL EMIL FRANZOS

TRANSLATED FROM THE GERMAN BY

M. W. MACDOWALL

NEW YORK

D. APPLETON AND COMPANY

1, 3, AND 5 BOND STREET

1883

PREFACE

TO THE AMERICAN EDITION.

———

ALTHOUGH the high literary art which Franzos possesses (the finer quality of which has been preserved in this translation) is fully admitted by intelligent Jews, the subject-matter of his book itself, its *raison d'être*, they have by no means relished. In a review of "The Jews of Barnow," published some months ago in a leading New York journal, it was asserted by the writer that, from internal evidence, Franzos must be a Jew. This statement was directly controverted by a Jewish weekly of the highest standing. Still, we must believe that the acumen of the New York reviewer was not at fault, because in a late number of "Blackwood's Magazine," which contained an interesting criticism of Franzos and his book, it was asserted that the author is or was a Jew. No man not born a Jew, perfectly familiar with all the phases of Jewish life in Eastern Galicia, and in sympathy with them, could have created this book.

Franzos may have clothed Jews and Jewesses with poetical raiment, given them melodramatic phrasings, but the gabardine, caftan, love-locks, are visible—the whine, the nasal twang audible.

This denial that Franzos was a Jew, though apparently insignificant in itself, and due, perhaps, to a want of acquaintance with the facts, is still peculiarly indicative of a natural *travers* of the Jewish mind. Any description of the inner life of Jews, when written by a Jew, unless it be laudatory, is particularly distasteful to Jews. No race cares to have its failings exposed. From one of another creed such strictures may be passed over with stolid indifference, but, from one of their own blood, any censure, direct or applied, is considered by Jews in the light of a sacrilege. With Jews it is ever a cry, "It is a dirty bird that fouls its own nest." Such acridity as a Goldwin Smith distills, Jews laugh at ; but when one of their kinsmen, a Mr. Montefiore, finds fault with them, bidding them look for grace in another direction, then at once a holy horror pervades them.

What Franzos describes is Jewish life pent up within the narrow limits of some Galician town. Religious dislikes, racial hatreds kindled a thousand years ago, have never been quenched. Though to-day in that town a Jew could not be murdered, because it would be against the law, the inclination to kill him, because he is a Jew, still exists. The simple fact, that every Jew had been taught to read and write, had quickened his brains. Through heredity he became, intellectually, superior to the illiterate peasant, or townsfolk, who hemmed him in. The mental phenomenon the Jew would present, under such conditions, would not be, after all, so peculiar. He had but two ends in life, to work and pray. Even his toil was restricted, for he could only engage in certain callings. His solace was his religion. He might pray to his Maker, but only in such set phrases as had been chosen for him. His God was by far too sublime for him, poor worm, to address in such homely words as might well up spontaneously from his own heart. A slave to tradition, bound down by rote, the Jew had been taught that the least divergence from a cut-and-dried ritual was heresy. Mental and physical isolation brought about arrested development. The only wonder about this all is, that the Jew in Eastern Europe, seeing a better chance for life beyond the pale of his religion, had not broken bounds, and, abjuring his creed, found outside of it an easier existence. Brushing aside that sentimentalism which so often obscures considerations of this character, the chances of security for an apostate Jew were not very certain. Travestied in the guise of a Christian, he never could have looked like one. Stamped on his features were all the marked characteristics of his Orientalism. Even his tongue would have played him false, for the rabbi had forbidden him the use of that language common to the state in which he lived. By some complications brought about by the Jews themselves in Eastern Europe, they are not always subjected to the same regulations as Christians. Religious laws made for their own government, which underpinned their social life, were rarely meddled with. In a primitive society, necessarily ignorant, any accredited head, according to the laws of sociology, must be a despotic one. A rabbi, then, in these unknown towns, wielded almost the power of life and death. That modern infliction of Boycotting has been borrowed directly from the Jews. For a trivial divergence from common custom the punishment was severe. In these Polish or Russian districts, thirty years ago, a Jew did not dare read a Christian book.

What Franzos shows markedly in his "Jews of Barnow" is that barrier which Jews throw around their household. The seclusion of the family, so purely Oriental in its character, is something which the Polish rabbi takes particular pains to teach. This hiding, of what is the finest trait the Jew possesses, that love and peace which dwell in his home, that reverence which children have for their parents, that sacrifice of everything to his affections, because it never is known, has tended more than anything else to alienate the Jew from his neighbor. Among the ultra-orthodox Jews, whether they live in Odessa, Cracow, Frankfort, London, or New York, their doors are inhospitably closed to those of another belief. Has there been transmitted some instinct engendered by mistrust?

Is Judaism, then, so sensitive a plant that it should wither by mere contact? If, to live, it must have seclusion, it approaches closely to the Eastern's idea of a woman's virtue, something wanting the protection of high walls and difficult approaches. In our age, any religion which requires exclusiveness so that it may exist is hardly worth the keeping.

Franzos's stories exhibit those barbarities even now practiced under the sacred name of religion. There are Jews who are not merely galled by the opprobrium which in some places is still attached to their race, but are sincerely desirous of removing it. Franzos, because he describes what is the iron law of Talmudical or rabbinical tradition, shows how superstition degrades the man. It is difficult at this day, when research and modern methods of criticism have thrown such a flood of light on the past, to realize the mental condition of that vast body of Jews at the time of the commencement of the Christian era and the destruction of Jerusalem. The whole national and municipal administration of the country was in the hands of the priesthood. Every law, every ordinance, every police and sanitary regulation, became a religious obligation. Every action in every man's family, whether social or political, was regulated for him by rules handed down from former generations, and these rules were barnacled by conventionalisms. For his guidance in the most commonplace actions, a Jew had perforce recourse to his rabbi. As must always be the case, when municipal administration emanates from a church, religious observances override legal or social obligations. With the crucifixion of Christ came that hatred of Jews, the intensity of which can only now be measured by its continuance. The exclusion of Jews from the society and communion of mankind petrified into marble-like hardness all those existing traditions which guided the Jew's methods of life. Forbidden by every conceivable form of oppression and disability from accompanying the rest of mankind on their march toward a higher civilization, every advance, mental or physical, denied them, it was as if a hot iron had been seared over the bloody wound which had lopped them off from the family of nations. It is a wonder that all future growth was not arrested. As to the charge of tribalism (the writer acknowledging that the vast majority of Jews believe in it), and even according some unknown and undefined power as derivable from tribalism, to make a charge of this is but to repeat the old fable of the wolf and the lamb.

All that intelligent Jews are doing to-day is to take advantage of their freedom. They are trying to rid themselves of that incubus which has been weighing them down. That large and increasing number of Reformers and Reform synagogues, springing up in the large cities of Western Europe and the United States; the decadence, the difficulty of maintaining synagogues of pure orthodox Jews; the complaints, the lamenta-

tions which are constantly heard from the mouths of orthodox ministers and their organs, over what they call
"the neglect of religious observance," show that the
time of change has come.   Even among some of the orthodox, the gross superstitions accompanying the offer-
ings (auction-sales of God's blessings, knocked down to
the highest bidder) have been for the major part abol-
ished.   Efforts are continually made to modify the ritual
by denationalizing the older-fashioned form of prayer,
and giving it more of that spiritual life which Maimoni-
des first developed.   Dietary and physical observances,
which the Eastern Jew borrowed or adopted from the
nations which once surrounded him, are being ex-
punged.

What is the true reason for this change, a change
which, born in America and in England, is now com-
mencing to exert some slight influence in Germany?
The blood of the martyrs is the seed of the Church.
Every act of wrong done to Jews rendered them the
more rigid in their belief, causing at the same time dif-
ferentiation in their surroundings.   Whenever, through
the operation of better, more humane laws, oppression
was removed, Jews became more like the men among
whom they lived.   Why should M. Renan find fault with
the French Jew, and take the Parisian Israelite as the
type of some Hebraic Athenian?   Under normal conditions men float in the general current, at about equal
depths, for the social law of specific gravity remains

forever the same. Those sociologists are ignorant of
their calling who demand, then, of the Jew an instanta-
neous reversal of an existence formed by his surroundings, and a forgetting of the great belief which has been
burned into his heart by the fires of thousands of years.

To the American Jew, "The Jews of Barnow" shows
very clearly a great many things he may have been ignorant about. Jews who came to this country fifty
years since, who by thrift, honesty, and intelligence,
have secured an ample store of the world's goods, are
prone to forget their early surroundings, or hesitate to
tell their American children of that bigotry which existed in their European birth-places. They have educated their children in their own creed ; but American
school-boys or school-girls have had one inestimable
blessing, the contact with an outer world and the opportunity of thinking for themselves. Education and
superstition can never have a co-existence. These fathers would feel ashamed, then, did they tell their children the absurdities which they once were taught.
That one story of Franzos's, "The Child of Atonement,"
is a revelation. As an American Jew reads it, he might
be inclined to deem the Rabbi of Sadagóra a Torque-
mada, or that it was a clever creation, having no existence save in the brain of the romance-writer. But it is
not a fancy-drawn picture, but had once actual being.
Such stories as "The Child of Atonement" and "The
Nameless Graves" can not be read by any intelligent

Jew without the burning brand of shame rising to his cheeks. As to the truthfulness of many portions of Franzos's book, unfortunately there can be no possible doubt. There may not be many Rabbis of Sadagóra, but excommunication, the *cherem*, that social inquisition, is as prevalent in Russia and Poland, in 1882, as it was a thousand years ago. The Rabbi of Sadagóra of Franzos's book is dead, but his son actually lives, exercises perhaps not the same cruelties, but attributes to himself the identical miraculous functions as did his wicked father before him, and still this younger medicine-man has his followers.

"The Jews of Barnow" should make the existence of a Rabbi of Sadagóra an impossibility. Jewish women who read "The Jews of Barnow" will be amazed to learn how degraded is the condition of their sex in Eastern Europe. That one horrible text in their prayer-book, said by the men, "Thank God that thou hast not made me a woman," belongs to the period of the coarsest barbarity. It is incorporated in innumerable volumes, now perhaps being printed. Educated Jews who read this vicious paragraph, who think of mother, wife, and daughter, feel the degradation of it, and loathe its interpretation. We can not agree with Frances Power Cobbe in the general application of this sentence of hers, that "something appears to be lacking in Jewish feeling concerning women. Too much of Oriental materialism still lingers. Too little of Occidental chivalry and romance has yet arisen." This might be applicable for the East, even in its most exaggerated sense, but is hardly just to the West. Still, as Franzós tells us in his book, girls are sold to men, and become, it is true, wives, but with as little ceremony as if they were Circassians.

The oldest source of any religion is not the purest, "If it be an historical religion, fanaticism always assumes the form of a return to the primitive type." The ultra-orthodox Jew is ruled by the Ashkenazim of Jerusalem, the most superstitious, the most ignorant of men. This sect still fights for power. Even the purity of the Ashkenazim's belief, monotheism, the only thing left it, must be taken with suspicion, because the sanity or sincerity of any Cabalist is to be doubted.

There are little, if any, differences existing in the social strata, educated or uneducated, which uphold Christian beliefs. If Rome is the fountain-head of Catholicity, Jerusalem ought to be the true source whence Hebraism flows. The Holy City of the Jews does exert its influence over millions of the ultra-orthodox, but for educated Israelites has no more weight than have the decrees of any miracle-working rabbi who holds forth in Cracow. If there be in Russia, Finland, Scandinavia, Austria, Hungary, Roumania, Turkey, some five and a half million Jews, and in England, France, and the United States, half a million more, what a vast proportion are steeped in darkness!

What does as much as anything else to injure the Jew, and to make mankind his enemy, is that belief he entertains that he is the race "God cherishes most." This is, indeed, tribalism. Selected by the Creator as his special favorites, pious Jews think that to them "all blessings shall be given." Once it was believed that a Jew's brain was made of a finer material, that he was less subject to dementia, than others. Some very sad personal observations assure the writer that such is not the case. If anything, in that struggle for wealth in which Jews engage in the large cities of the United States, they have children more prone to feeble-mindedness than Christians. The close-marriage system of the Jews may in a certain measure induce degeneracy by exhaustion of the original stock, for the laws of nature are inexorable, and act alike in Christian or Mohammedan. That preservation of his race is something the Jew most particularly prides himself about. The Parsee, who for so long a time has had a religion apart, presents the precise condition of an isolated existence which the Jew is so proud of. Morality, continence, the sacred character of the marriage-ties, do in a certain measure preserve the Jewish race, but the miraculous in such fractional existence has nothing marvelous about it. This self-laudation of race, that "pride-belief," is the most difficult to eradicate, for it has been the consolation of an oppressed race.

What, then, is reform, this Jewish reform? It is

pure, unadulterated monotheism.   It believes that men,
though they may expound religion, can not create it.
It looks on the Talmud, as did Emanuel Deutsch, as the
most poetical, the most confusing of chronicles, but
utterly worthless for the guidance of any human
being—a curiosity, patched over, embroidered, by a
thousand different hands, something to be placed in a
cabinet, to be gazed on, but as practically useless for
human instruction as would be the Arthurian romances.
Yayha ibn Main was a worshiper of the Prophet, and
labored all his life to purify the text of his Koran, and
thus he is recorded to have said : "I wrote down numbers of traditions under the dictation of liars, and made
use of the paper for heating my ovens.   I thus obtained at least one advantage—my bread was well-
baked."   One saying in the Talmud is applicable to it :
"They dived into the ocean and brought up a pot-
sherd."   Oh, the *olla-podrida* of nonsense in it !   And
still it shapes the lives of millions of Jews ; it warps
their ways, for it is almost their only book.

The Reformer is no iconoclast, he is educated enough
not to wish to destroy this relic of a past, but he is
striving to expunge it, to deprive the Talmud from ex-
erting its baleful influence.   The reformed Jew believes
in a God of mercy—one of love.   He thinks that his
Creator is not a vengeful being.   He does not believe
that Christ was the Son of God, doubts even a coming
Messiah, but thinks that modern teachings have done

for man's immortal soul what the older lawgivers did
for grosser flesh and blood only.   What the Reformer
desires most especially is that he shall have readers,
clergymen (call them what you please), who shall not
only be familiar with the language they live in, but
have the highest, the very highest education, be in fact
the equals of those who preach to their Christian friends.
These Reformers sicken over those attempts of crass
ignorance which, through the borrowed sanctity of a
salaried office, assume the direction of educated intelligence.   The majority of these Reformers are utterly
indifferent to dietary regulations.   Can peace with God,
a resurrection of the soul after the death of the body,
entrance to heaven, have anything to do with the eating
of a mollusk ?   Could the great Creator have made food
for one man which another dare not eat ?   Trivialities,
mixed up in religion, debase it, weaken it, sap it to its
very vitals.   A stronger, more hearty belief must
emancipate itself from puerilities.   A reformed Jew
can not be a materialist, though he may strip religion
of its symbolisms.

Millennium is far distant, and a Bishop of Sadagóra
and a Goldwin Smith may never, perhaps, lie in the same
bed, or sup at the same banquet, for both of them represent that antagonism which inflamed England in King
John's time, or is rampant to-day with Pastor Stöcker
in King William of Prussia's reign.   "Every country
has the Jews it deserves," writes Franzos, quoting the

most direful of sayings. God help, in his infinite mercy, American-born Jews if, in generations to come, this cruel speech had ever an application! It might arise from their own errors, and the faults of their surroundings. It would mean, however, nothing less than the political degradation of that country in which Christian and Jew live. Mr. Froude has been much blamed, little lauded, for what he wrote in regard to an oppressed race. It was somewhat as follows: that those who could not fight for their freedom did not deserve it.

It sometimes happens that fiction produces effects where facts fail. It is believed, then, that Franzos's stories will not only be of interest to numerous readers, but in the hands of the reformed Jew, by means of the lessons it teaches, help him in his earnest efforts to save his race from retrogression.

BARNET PHILLIPS.

PREFACE.

THE following stories, the scene of which is laid in the Podolian Ghetto, were my first literary attempt. They were for the most part written while I was at the university, and were published in various journals. Owing to circumstances, another and later book—"Aus Halb-Asien"—was the first to come out; for this youthful work was not published as a whole until 1876. I mention this, although it is visible from internal evidence, to explain my choice of subjects. The preface to that edition gives a further account of this, and from it I make the following quotations :

"When I took up my pen four years ago, I strongly felt the necessity of making my work as artistic as possible. I wished to write stories, and strove to give them poetic value. For this very reason, it seemed necessary that I should describe the kind of life with which I was best acquainted. This was essentially the case with regard to that of the Podolian Jews. I therefore became the historian of the Podolian Ghetto, and it was my great desire to give these stories an artistic form; but not at the cost of truth. I have never permitted my love of the beautiful to lead me into the sin of falsifying the facts and conditions of life, and am confident that I have described this strange and outlandish mode of existence precisely as it appeared to me. If in my first published volume my efforts to portray men and manners needed the assistance of my powers as a novelist, so in this book my knowledge of men and manners has to help me in my labors as a novelist. Sometimes the one side of my character takes the upper hand, and sometimes the other; but still they are at bottom inseparable, and it has always been my endeavor to describe facts artistically. However the novelist may be judged, the portrayer of men and manners demands that his words should be believed.

"This request is not superfluous, for it is a very strange mode of life to which I am about to introduce the reader. The influences and counter-influences that affect it are only touched upon in this book. Had I given a full account of them in an introduction, the introduction would in all likelihood have been longer than the book. I have therefore refrained from doing it, and believe that I was right in making this decision. For I have kept before my eyes, while penning these stories, that I am writing for a Western reader. If he will only trust to my love of truth, and regard the separate stories in combination with each other, he will gain a clear idea of the kind of life I describe without any further particulars. I would repeat one sentence, the truth of which is shown in my first book: 'Every country has the Jews that it deserves'—and it is not the fault of the Polish Jews that they are less civilized than their brethren in the faith in England, Germany, and France. At least, it is not entirely their fault.

"No one can do more than his nature permits. This book is to a certain extent polemical, and the stories are written with an object. I do not deny that this is the case, and do not think it requires any excuse. Still I have never allowed myself to sin against truth in the pursuit of this object. I do not make the Polish Jews out to be either better or worse than they really are. These stories are not written for the purpose of holding up the Eastern Jews to obloquy or admiration, but with the object of throwing as much light as I could in dark places."

The second edition, published in 1877, only differed from the first in a few alterations made in the language; but the third edition (from which this translation is taken) is not only enlarged, but is also changed in several important particulars. I examined each story carefully, and strove to bring all into a distinct connection with each other, thus giving a clear idea of Polish Judaism regarded as a whole. For this reason new tales were introduced: they describe Jewish customs that had been at first passed over in silence, but which were necessary for the proper appreciation of the subject.

This work has been translated into all European languages, as well as into Hebrew; and now I have the pleasure of being able to lay it before the English public, by whom I hope it will receive as kind a reception as it has been given elsewhere. I hope so less for my own sake than in the interest of the unfortunate people whose life it describes.

KARL EMIL FRANZOS.

VIENNA.

CONTENTS.

THE SHYLOCK OF BARNOW.

(1873.)

2

THE SHYLOCK OF BARNOW.

The Jew's great white house stands exactly opposite the old gray monastery of the Dominicans, and close to the public road that leads from Lemberg to Skala, passing through the gloomy little town of Barnow on the way. The people born in the small dirty houses of the Ghetto grow up with a feeling of the deepest respect and admiration for this house and its owner, old Moses Freudenthal. Both house and man are the pride of Barnow; and both in their own way justify this pride.

To describe the house in the first place. It really seems to be conscious of its own grandeur as it stands there proud and stately in all the dignity of white-washed cleanliness, the long windows of the first floor bright and shining, and the painted shutters of the shop-windows coming down to the very ground at either side of the great folding-doors which stand invitingly open. For it is a house of entertainment, and the nobles of the country-side know how to take ad-

vantage of its superior attractions when they come to
town on magisterial business, or attend the weekly
market. It is also patronized by the cavalry officers
who are stationed in the villages in the neighborhood, whenever the boredom of country quarters drives
them into town. Besides this, the house is let in
suites of apartments, and the greatest of the magnates of Barnow, such as the district judge and the
doctor, live there. But it would be difficult to give
a list of all the house contains, the ground-floor is
so crowded. In one room is a lottery agency, then
come the offices of a company for insuring cattle,
men, and corn ; and again, a drapery establishment,
a grocer's shop, a room in which gentlemen may
drink their wine, and another where the poor man can
enjoy his glass of brandy-and-water. But then, the
lottery agent, the agent of the insurance company,
the draper, the grocer, and the innkeeper are one
and all—Moses Freudenthal.

But the tall stern-looking old man to whom the
house belongs is even more worthy of notice than it
and all it contains. His family has been the grand-
est in the town as long as people can remember, and
to him belongs of right the chief place in the synagogue. His father had been appointed head of the
session on the death of his grandfather, and when his
father died he was chosen as his successor without a
dissentient voice, and by the unsolicited vote of the

whole congregation. He is regarded as one of the most pious and honorable men in the Jewish community. Added to this is his wealth—his enormous wealth!

His co-religionists regard him as a millionaire, and they are right. For he not only possesses the big white house and all that is in it, but he has every reason to look upon several of the estates in the neighborhood as more really belonging to him than to the Polish nobles who live on them. And then Komorowka is his also. This beautiful place fell into his hands when little Count Smólski and his lovely wife Aurora lost it by their extravagance after a very few years' possession. Komorowka is indeed a lovely place. No wonder that when the time came for Count Smólski to leave his old home, he was in such utter despair that he sought to forget his woes in the worst fit of drunkenness of his whole life.

Would you be much surprised if you were now told that Moses Freudenthal was not only the richest and proudest, but also the most envied, man in Barnow?

But this he is not. Ask the poorest man in the Jewish town—the teacher of the law, who, with his six children, often suffers from the pangs of hunger, or the water-carriers, who groan under the heavy pails they bear from morning to night from the town-well—ask these men whether they would exchange

lots with Moses, and they will at once answer, "No."
For Freudenthal's sorrow is even greater than his
wealth.

It is true that you can not read this in his face
as he stands, tall and stately, in the doorway of his
house. His silver-gray hair falls down below his black
velvet skull-cap ; the two long curls that hang, one
at each side of the face, as is the fashion of the
Chassidim, are also silver-gray and thin. But his figure is still strong and upright, and the curiously cut
Jewish coat that he wears, resembling a *talar* in shape,
and made of black cloth, is by no means an unbecom-
ing garment. The old man stands almost motionless
watching the painter who is busy painting the doors
of the spirit-shop a bright arsenic green, with bottles,
glasses, and *bretzeln*,* in yellow and white upon the
green background. He seldom turns to acknowledge
the greeting of a passer-by, for but few people are
in the streets to-day. Now and then a group of
Ruthenian peasants may be seen reeling out of the
town-gate, or a nobleman drives past in his light britzska, or perhaps it is some poor peddler, who has been
wandering the whole week long from farm to farm
in the district, exchanging money and cloth for the
sheepskins, laden with which he is returning to town.
His burden is heavy and his gain is but small, yet
his pale, worn, and, it may be, cunning face is not

* A kind of biscuit.

without a gleam of joy and pride. A few hours later and the miserable ragged Jewish peddler, on whom farmers and nobles had tried the weight of their whips, and on whom they had made many a scurrilous jest, is transformed into a proud prince awaiting the arrival of his lovely bride—the day of rest, the Sabbath.

He has not long to wait now, the Friday afternoon is drawing to a close, and the sun will soon set. Preparations for the day of rest are being made in every house; the sunlit street is almost totally deserted. Herr Lozinski, the district judge, a tall, thin, yellow-faced man, is coming down the street accompanied by a young stranger. He stands at the door for a few minutes talking to Moses before going upstairs to his rooms. They discuss the badness of the times, the low price of silver, and the promising April weather; for it is a real spring day, more like May than anything else. The streets are very dry, except for a few puddles in the market-place; the air is deliciously soft and warm, and yonder in the monk's garden the fruit-trees and elder bushes are covered with blossom. The Christian children coming home from school are shouting, "Spring! spring is coming!" "Yes, spring is coming," says the district judge, taking off his hat and leading his guest upstairs. "Spring is coming," repeats old Moses, passing his hand across his forehead as if awakening from a dream. . . . "Spring is coming!"

"Old Moses is a very remarkable man," says the district judge to the new registrar. "I scarcely know whether to call him eccentric or not. You won't believe it, but he knows as much law as the best barrister in the land. And besides that, he's the richest man in the country-side. He is said to be worth millions! And yet he slaves week-in, week-out, as though he hadn't the wherewithal to buy his Sabbath dinner."

"A niggardly money-grubber like all the Jews," says the registrar, making the smoke of his cigar curl slowly in the air.

"H'm! By no means. He is generous. I must confess that he is very generous. But his generosity gives him no more pleasure than his wealth. Yet he goes on speculating as before. And for whom, if you please—for whom?"

"Has he no children?" inquires the other.

"Yes. That's to say, he has and he hasn't. Ask him, and he will tell you that he has none. But you don't know his story, do you? . . . Every one here knows it—but then, you see, you come from Lemberg. I suppose that you never heard any one speak of the old man's daughter, beautiful Esther Freudenthal, when you were there? The whole affair is very romantic; I must tell it you. . . ."

The old man, whose story every one knows, is still leaning against the doorway of his house, watching the flower-laden branches of the fruit-trees in the cloister garden as they sway in the breeze. What is he thinking of? It can not be of his business; for his eyes are wet with unshed tears, and his lips tremble for a moment as though with stifled grief. He shades his eyes with his hand, as if the sunlight were blinding him. Then he draws himself up, and shakes his head, as though trying to rid himself of the sad thoughts that oppress him.

"Make haste, the Sabbath is drawing nigh," he says to the painter as he approaches to examine his work more closely.

The little humpback, who wears a shabby frogged coat of a fashion only known in Poland, has just finished the folding-doors, and now limps away to the window-shutters, paint-pot in hand. These shutters had formerly been colored a bright crimson, and their faded surface still bears the almost illegible inscription in white letters : "For ready money to-day —to-morrow gratis." Their glory has long since departed, and the little man, quickly filling his brush with the vivid green, begins to paint over them, saying as he works, "Do you remember, Pani Moschko, that I painted this too?" and with that he points to the dirty brown-red of the first coloring.

But Moses is thinking of other things, and scarcely heeding him, answers with an indifferent, "Really."

"Of course I did," continues the little man eagerly.

"Don't you remember? I painted it fifteen years ago on just such another beautiful day as this is. The house was quite new, and I was a young fellow then. When I had finished my work, you looked at it, and said, 'I am pleased with you, Janko.' You were standing in front of the door, just where you are now, I verily believe, and your little Esterka was beside you. Holy Virgin! how lovely the child was! And how pleasant it was to hear her laugh when she saw the white letters appearing one after the other on the red ground! She asked what they meant, the darling! You gave me three Theresien *zwanzigers* * for my work. I remember it as distinctly as if it were yesterday. I thought then that it was my last job in Barnow; for old Herr von Polanski wanted to send me to the school of design at Cracow. But soon afterward he lost every farthing he possessed, and was even obliged to sell his daughter Jadwiga in order to get food to eat, and so I remained a house-painter. Ah yes! man proposes and . . . . Deuce take it! The old man's gone, and here I am gossiping away to the empty air. I suppose that the Jew is counting his money as usual. . . ."

But Janko is mistaken. Moses Freudenthal is not counting his treasures at this moment. Indeed he would probably give up all that he possesses without a sigh could he thereby rid his life of what has made

* About 1s. 8d. English.

him poorer and more wretched than the beggar at
his gates. He has taken refuge in the large dusky
sitting-room, into which no ray of sunlight, and no
sound of the human voice, can penetrate. He can
now throw himself into his arm-chair, and sob from
the bottom of his heart without any one asking him
what is the matter; he can let his head fall upon his
breast, tear his hair, or cover his face with his hands.
. . . He does not weep, or pray, nor yet does he curse;
he moans out in pain, the words echoing in the quiet
room, "How pleasant it was to hear the child's
laugh!" . . . Thus he sits alone in the twilight. At
last he gets up and raises his eyes as if in prayer—
nay, rather as a man who demands a right. "O
God!" he cries, "I do not ask that she may come
back to me, for I made my servants drive her from
my door; I do not ask that she may be happy, for
she has sinned grievously in the sight of God and
man; I do not ask that she may be unhappy, for she
is my own flesh and blood; I only ask that she may
die, so that I may not have to curse my only child.
Let her die, O God, let her die, or let me! . . ."

Meanwhile the district judge is concluding his
story in the room above. "No one knows what has
become of the pretty little girl. She is forgotten;
her father even doesn't seem to remember her existence. They're a heartless race these Jews; they're
all alike. . . ."

It has grown dusk in the town, but there is no gloom in the hearts of its Jewish inhabitants. The dismal irregularly built houses of the Ghetto are now enlivened by thousands of candles, and thousands of happy faces. The Sabbath has begun in the hearts of these people and in their rooms, a common and usual occurrence, and yet a mysterious and blessed influence that drives away all that is poor and mean in everyday life. To-day, every hovel is lighted up, and every heart made glad with sufficiency of food. The teacher of the law has forgotten his hunger, the water-carrier his hard work, the peddler the blows and derision that continually fall to his lot, and the rich usurer his gain. To-day all are equal; all are the happy trustful sons of the same Almighty Father. The feeble light of the tallow-candle in its rude candlestick, and the soft light of the wax-candle in the silver candelabra, illumine the same picture. The daughters of the house and the little boys sit silently watching their mother, as she, in obedience to the beautiful old custom handed down from generation to generation, blesses the candles. The father then takes the large prayer-book down from the book-shelf and gives it to his eldest son to carry to the synagogue for him. After that they all go out into the street, the men and women keeping apart, as the strict law commands. Their words are few, and those they utter are grave and quiet. To-day neither grief nor joy finds vent in speech, for all hearts are full of the divine peace of the Sabbath. . . .

The large white house opposite the Dominican monastery is also illuminated. But the candles were lighted by a stranger, for there is no mistress there to speak the customary blessing. The finest linen covers the tables in the best parlor, which is handsomely furnished, but no child's merry laugh, and no loving word is heard there. The melancholy sound of the sputtering candles alone disturbs the stillness.

But the old man who now enters the room in his Sabbath suit has been accustomed to this state of things for years—for five long years. At first he used involuntarily to turn and listen for the sound of the voice he loved so well ; for it was on an evening such as this that his child had left him. But this evening he crosses the room quickly, and taking the heavy leather-bound prayer-book from the shelf, leaves the room at once. Does he fear that to-day of all days the ghosts of the past will come forth to meet him from every corner of the well-lighted room ?

If that be the case, it is foolish to fly from them, Moses Freudenthal ! See, they dog your footsteps wherever you go through the narrow gloomy little streets. They whisper in your ear, even though you strive to drown their voices by entering into conversation with the passers-by. They appear before your very eyes in spite of your fixing them upon the votive

tablets fastened to the pillars in the house of God !
And when you pass through the congregation and take
your seat in your accustomed place, they flutter around
your head, look at you out of the very letters of your
prayer-book, and speak to you in the voice of the offi-
ciating minister ! . . .

"Praise ye the Lord. Break out into joy, glad-
ness, and song. For He judgeth the world with right-
eousness and the people with His truth."

"And the solitary," cries a secret voice in the heart
of the unhappy man, "shall He break in pieces ! " His
eyes are fixed upon his book, his lips whisper the words
of prayer ; but he does not pray, he can not ! The
whole of his past life rises ghost-like before his mental
vision, and in such vivid detail as to cause him intense
agony. . . .

"He who can no longer pray," his old father had
often told him, and now the words involuntarily recur
to him,—" He who can no longer pray shall be cast out
from before the face of the Eternal." He distinctly
remembers the day on which he had first heard those
words. He was then a boy of thirteen, and had been
allowed to put on the phylacteries for the first time,
the sign that he had reached man's estate. The life
that opened out before him on that day was not easy
and pleasant like that of the fortunate of the earth, but
hard and narrow as that endured by his race. In common with every one around him, he had early learned

to dedicate his life to two objects, and these were—
prayer and money-making. When he was seventeen
years of age, his father had called him into his room,
and had then told him, in a calm matter-of-fact tone,
that he was to marry Chaim Grünstein's daughter
Rosele in three months' time. He did not know the
girl. He had seen her, it is true, but he had never
really looked at her. His father had, however, chosen
her to be his wife, and he was satisfied that it was well.
Three months later he married Rosele. . . .

Hark! the Chazzân is beginning the ancient Sabbath hymn, whose words, expressive of joy and longing, go straight to the heart—"Lecho daudi likras
kalle." And immediately the choir takes up the strain
triumphantly, "Lecho daudi likras kalle"—"Come, O
friend, let us go forth to meet the Bride, let us receive
the Sabbath with joy!"

Strange emotion to stir the spirit of a people to its
very depths! Strange that all the passion and sen-
suousness of which its heart and mind are capable are
expended on the adoration of the Divinity, and on that
alone. The same race whose genius gave birth to the
Song of Songs—the eternal hymn of love,—and to
whom the world owes the story of Ruth, the most
beautiful idyl of womanhood ever known—has now,
after a thousand years of the night of oppression and
wandering, learned to look upon marriage as a mere
matter of business, by which to secure some pecuniary

advantage, and as a means of preventing the chosen of
the Lord from dying off the face of the earth. These
men know not what they do—they have no suspicion
of the sin of which they are guilty in thus acting.

Nor did Moses Freudenthal know it. He honored
his wife as long as she lived, and found in her a
faithful helpmeet in joy and sorrow. A blessing
seemed to rest upon everything he did, for whatever
he undertook prospered. He studied the language of
the Christians around him with an eager determination to learn, and then began the arduous task of
learning German law: the man of thirty studied as
hard as if he had been a schoolboy. He was not actu-
ated by the desire of gain alone, but also by a love
of honor and knowledge. And this knowledge bore
fruit; he became rich—very rich. The nobles and
officers of the neighborhood came to his house and
bowed themselves down before the majesty of his
wealth; but before he had done with them, they were
forced to hold him in as much respect as his gold.
In those days every one envied him, and people used
to whisper as he passed—"That is the happiest man
in the whole district."

But was he really happy? If he were so, why
did he often look gloomy, and why did Rosèle weep
as if her heart would break, when she was sure that
no one could see her? A dark shadow rested on the
married life of this couple, who, in their daily inter-

course, had gradually learned to esteem each other.
Their marriage was childless. As they had been
brought together by strangers, and were not even yet
united in heart and soul, they could not live down
their sorrow, or find comfort in each other's love.
The proud man bore his grief in silence, and, unmoved, watched his wife fading away before his very
eyes. When his friends spoke of a divorce, he shook
his head, but no word of love for the unhappy woman
to whom he was bound ever crossed his lips. Years
passed away; but at last one evening—it was in
winter—when he entered the sitting-room, and wished
his wife "good evening" as usual, instead of answer-
ing softly, and glancing at him shyly and sadly, she
hastened to meet him, and clung to him as though
she felt for the first time that she had a right to his
love. He gazed at her blushing excited face, his surprise giving way to joyful anticipation; then taking
her hand, he drew her down to the seat beside him,
and made her lay her head upon his breast. Their
lips trembled, but neither of them could find words
to express their joy—none seemed adequate! . . .

"Praise ye the Lord!" These words of the minister roused Moses from his dream of the past, and
he hears the congregation reply, "Praised be the
Lord our God, who createth the day and createth
the night, who separateth the light from the darkness, and the darkness from the light: praised be

the Lord, the Almighty, the Eternal, the God of
battles ! . . ."

"Praised be God !" . . . With what mixed
feelings had Moses Freudenthal joined in this cry of
thanksgiving on that Sabbath evening twenty-two
years ago when he first entered the house of God a
father ! His heart bled and rejoiced at the same
moment ; he wept with mingled joy and sorrow, for
a little daughter had indeed been born to him : but
his wife's strength had been unable to withstand her
sufferings, and she had died. She had borne her
terrible agony with unmurmuring resignation ; and
even when dying a happy smile passed over her pale
face whenever she heard the voice of her child. In
those sad hours before the end the hearts of the husband and wife, that had remained strangers to each
other during the long years of their married life, at
length found each other out. He alone understood
why his wife said, "Now I can die in peace ;" she
alone understood why he bent over her hand again
and again, sobbing, "Forgive me, Rosele ; forgive
me !" "The child," she said ; "take care of the
child !" then she shivered and died. Next morning
they carried her out to the "good place." And he
rent his garments, took the shoes from off his feet,
and sat on the floor of the chamber of death for seven
days and seven nights, thus fulfilling the days of
mourning after the manner of the children of Israel.

He did not weep, but fixed his sad tearless eyes on
the flame of the funeral light which has to burn for
a whole week, in order that the homeless spirit may
have a resting - place on earth until God shows it
where it is henceforth to dwell.

"He is talking to the dead," whispered his relations in awe-struck tones, when they saw his lips
move, as he murmured, "All might have been well
now, and you are dead ! "

His sorrow found relief in tears when they brought
him the child, and asked what it should be called.
"Esther," he answered—"Esther, like my mother."
He held his little daughter long in his arms, and his
tears fell on her face. Then he gave the child back
to her nurse, and from that moment became calm
and composed.

When the days of mourning were over he returned
to his business, and worked harder than ever before.
A new spirit seemed to possess him, and every day he
embarked in new and daring undertakings. He ventured to do what no one else would attempt, and fortune remained true to him. He now carried out the
wish he had long nourished—bought the piece of land
opposite the Dominican monastery, and began to build
a large house there. He passed his days in unceasing
labor ; but in the evening he would sit for hours at a
time by his child's cradle, gazing at the soft baby face.
And in the first months after his bereavement, the

nurse was often startled by seeing him come noiselessly into the nursery in the middle of the night, and watch and listen long to see if all were well with the child.

The days grew into months, the months into years, and little Esterka became ever more remarkable for beauty and cleverness as time went on. She was very like her father, for she had the same black curly hair, high forehead, and determined mouth; but in strange and touching contrast with the other features of the defiant little face, were the gentle blue eyes she had inherited from her mother. The father often looked at those eyes, and whenever he did so, he took his little girl in his arms, pressed her to his heart, and called her by a thousand pet names; but except at such times, the grave reserved man showed the child few tokens of the almost insane love he bore her.

When Esther was five years old they left the small house they had formerly inhabited in the Ghetto, and went to live in the large white house opposite the monastery. And after that Moses began to take measures for the education of his daughter, who was to be brought up according to old established usage. Esther learned to cook, to pray, and to count—that was enough for the house, for heaven, and for life. And what could her father have taught her in addition to this? Polish and German, perhaps? She could speak both languages, and he, like every other Jew in Barnow, regarded reading and writing as needless luxuries for a girl. He had learned both in order that he might write his business letters, and understand the book of civil law ; his daughter did not need to do either. Besides that, would greater knowledge make her a better or happier woman ? "When a Jewish girl knows how to pray"—has come to be a proverb among these stern-natured men—"she needs nothing more to make her good and happy !" And yet little Esther was to learn to read German, and much more besides ! . . .

"It was in an hour of weakness," murmurs the old man, as he rises with the rest of the congregation to take part in the long prayer, during which all must stand—"of weakness and folly that I gave way. Woe unto me for consenting, and cursed be he who led me astray ! "

"How can you say so, Moses Freudenthal ! However much your misfortunes may have enlightened you, and taught you to know your own heart, you can not even yet see that it was a sin you were committing in shutting out the light of the world from your child, and that you did right when you consented to permit another to reveal it to her. Oh, how you sin, old man, when, hardening your heart in egotism and ignorance, you say, "That was the cause of her misfortunes and of mine also ! From that time forward her mind was poisoned, and turned away from me and my God ! Cursed, cursed be that hour ! "

. . . But all this happened on a warm bright sum-

mer evening thirteen years ago. . . . The moonlight
lay on the houses and streets, and the very dust on
the road seemed to glitter like silver. Moses Freudenthal was sitting on the stone seat at his door lost in
thought. He felt strangely soft hearted that evening ;
for whether he would or not, he could not help living
over again in memory the occurrences of his former
life, and thinking of his dead wife Rosele. His
daughter, who was now nine years old, was sitting
beside him, gazing wide-eyed into the moonlit night.
Suddenly a man came up the street and stood looking
at them. Moses did not at once recognize him, but
little Esther sprang to her feet with a cry of joy—
"Uncle Schlome ! How glad I am that you have
come to see us, Uncle Schlome ! "

Moses now recognized the stranger, and rose in astonishment. What did Schlome Grünstein want with
him, and how had his daughter become acquainted
with the "Meschumed ?" He was Rosele's brother,
and had been his playfellow in his boyhood, but
Moses had not spoken to him for twenty years ; for a
pious Jew could hold no communication with a Meschumed, an apostate from the faith — and Schlome
was an apostate in the eyes of the Ghetto. And yet
the pale, delicate-looking man, with the gentle dreamy
expression, had always remained a Jew, and had lived
quietly and peacefully among his neighbors, spending
his wealth in works of charity and mercy. But the

name and the shame had cleaved to him from his
youth upward.

His had been a strange boyhood. As he had been
a shy, thoughtful child, living only in his books,
and showing no talent except in literary things, his father determined to make him a Rabbi. Schlome was
pleased with this decision, and studied so hard to fit
himself for his future calling that he not only injured
his health, but soon got beyond his teacher. The delicate boy was consumed by an unquenchable thirst for
knowledge. And this thirst became the cause of his
destruction, the curse of his life. By means of money
and passionate entreaties combined, he induced the
Christian schoolmaster of the place to teach him at
night and in secret. Thus he learned High German,
the forbidden and much-hated language of the Gentiles
around him, and also "Christian theology." Of the
latter branch of learning the schoolmaster himself
knew very little; so he helped out his ignorance by
lending his unwearied pupil many books belonging to
the Dominican library, and this he did before Schlome
had got over all the difficulties of learning to read.
In this way the boy read all manner of strange books,
one on the top of the other, and often enough, no
doubt, put sufficiently curious interpretations upon
them. At last one day a book fell into his hands,
which nearly drove him mad. The form and tone
were well known to him, for did they not enforce obe-

dience to the holy Thora (Law)? But the spirit that
breathed in its pages was another and—the youth's
very blood seemed to freeze in his veins—a milder and
better than what he had known. For this book was
the New Testament. Its teaching seemed to him like
the mild beauty of a spring day, and yet his hair
stood on end with horror. This, then, was the idol-
worship of the Christians,—this was the history of the
life and labors of that Man whom his father crucified,
and from whose likeness he had been taught to turn
away his head in hatred and contempt! The blow
was too severe. Schlome became very ill, and lay for
many weeks dangerously sick of a fever. Often and
often in his delirium the unconscious youth wept and
talked of the pale Nazarene, of the cross, and of that
ill-starred book. His parents and neighbors listened
to his ravings in horror; they searched into their
cause, and at length discovered Schlome's secret
studies. Soon afterward a strange rumor was circu-
lated in the Ghetto, to the effect that Schlome Grünstein had wished to become a Christian, and that as a
punishment for this sin God had visited him with madness. In course of time the youth recovered, and
went about among his brethren in the faith as usual;
but henceforth he seemed paler, shyer, and more
depressed than before. No one knew what inward
conflicts he had to wage; but every child in the
Jewish quarter called him a Meschumed, and told

how he had sworn a holy oath to his father that he
would only remain a Jew on two conditions—first,
that he might buy and read whatever books he chose ;
and second, that he might remain unmarried. He
kept his oath, even when the death of his parents
made him rich and independent. Thus he passed
his life in the narrow, gloomy Ghetto. He had only
one friend, David Blum, a man who devoted his life
to tending the sick, and whose own story was both
strange and sad. But then he did not make him
his friend till late in life, and lost him soon afterward ; for David Blum died, whether of low fever
or of a broken heart it were difficult to say. The
Meschumed mourned his loss deeply. It seemed
to him as though a bit of his own heart had been
buried with his friend. And yet these men differed
from each other as much in character as in the circumstances that had moulded their lives. David
was strong and high-hearted, but quick-tempered and
fantastic, so that he broke down once for all when
fate aimed a heavy blow at him ; Schlome, on the
contrary, was weak and gentle, and endowed with a
great power of endurance which enabled him to bend
under the blows of fate instead of being broken by
them. Thus he lived on in the midst of men and
yet terribly alone—the poor even hesitated to accept
charity at his hands. Still he loved all men, but
especially children ; and these alone returned his

affection, although they could seldom show it from
fear of their parents. He almost idolized little
Esther, the only child of his dead sister; and she
loved him better than her grave, reserved father.

Such was the man who came up to the bench on
which Moses Freudenthal and his daughter were
seated on that lovely summer evening.

"I want to speak to you, brother," he said, as
Moses rose and looked at him with a coldly question-
ing gaze. He then requested the child to go to bed,
and after she had left them, continued: "I want to
speak to you about many important things. Sit
down beside me. . . . You needn't be afraid!
There isn't a creature to be seen in the street. . . ."

Moses sat down hesitatingly.

"It is about the child," resumed the Meschumed.
"I have been thinking long and earnestly about her,
and when I chanced to see you this evening as I
was passing, I determined to say what I had to say
at once. You see, brother, the child is growing a
big girl. She will be beautiful one day; but what
is more to the purpose at present, is, that her goodness and intelligence are surprising in one so young.
You have scarcely any idea of the sort of questions
she asks, and of the kind of thoughts that little head
contains—you'd hardly believe it, brother."

"And how do you know?" interrupted Moses, in a
harsh stern voice. "Did I ever give you leave? . . ."

"Don't let us discuss that point, if you please," replied Schlome, raising his hand in deprecation, "don't let us discuss that point. I could answer you boldly that Esther is my sister's child, and that I have a right to love and care for her. But I will not answer you thus; we have been kept apart long enough by angry words. And even if you tell me that I am a stranger in your house, and by my own fault, too, I will answer you nothing. Love is not alone induced by ties of blood, and the world is not so rich in love that one can afford to cast any aside. But—it isn't that you mean. You fear danger for your child; you fear that I should try to undermine her faith. You feel less confidence in me than in the lowest servant in your house."

He ceased, but Moses made no reply. And yet the hard man's heart was really touched when he once more heard the voice that had been so dear to him in his boyhood. But he shook off his emotion, and when Schlome repeated his question, answered with cold severity, "My servants are all pious, and are stanch believers in the faith of their fathers." This he said with his eyes fixed on the ground. Had he looked up he would have seen his brother-in-law's lips tremble with bitter grief and disappointment. And yet his answer was gentle.

"Listen, Moses," he said; "it is written, and it is a true saying, 'By their fruits ye shall know

them.' Every incident of my life is known to you,
and to all our neighbors. I have always been terribly
alone in the world, forsaken of all men, but still I
have striven with all my heart and soul to unite my
life to that of others. I have striven to make it as
useful as it was possible for it to be after the blight
that had fallen upon it. You are the first person to
whom I have ever said this, and you will be the last
who will ever hear from me that I know I have
acted toward my fellow-men with as much beneficence—as it is called—as I could; and yet, what is
such beneficence in reality but the duty every man
owes to his kind? I have not, therefore, lived either
a happy or a good life; but judge, Moses, I entreat
of you, whether it shows either folly or sin?"

Moses passed his hand slowly across his forehead
and eyes, as though to give himself time for thought.

Then he answered more mildly:

"No man can judge a whole life with a righteous
judgment; God, who knows all, can alone do so. I
am willing to believe it is as you say, and it is well
for you that you can thus justify your life. For you
can thus wait quietly for the hour when God Himself
will judge you. But "—he interrupted himself, and then
continued, almost shyly—" *do* you believe in God?"

"Yes," replied Schlome, raising his head; yes, I
believe in Him. I sought Him in my boyhood, when
I imagined that he was a God of wrath and ven-

geance, the light and refuge of one people alone; I sought Him in my youth, when I imagined that He was a God of love and mercy, who yet was only gracious to those who worshiped Him with certain forms and ceremonies. Later on, I really found Him and knew Him as He is. He is neither a God of wrath nor of mercy, but a God of justice and necessity; He *is*, and all are in Him, even those who deny Him. . . ."

He had risen in his excitement, and as he stood in the moonlight before Moses, the latter felt strangely moved; it seemed to him almost as if Schlome's face shone. He did not know how it happened, but he could not help looking at the image of Christ opposite to him in the monastery garden, which stood out sharp and distinct in the clear pale light against the dark sky. "And He over there?" he asked, almost fearing the words he had uttered.

"He," answered the Meschumed, his voice sounding strangely soft and gentle, "He was a great and noble man, perhaps the best man that ever lived. But He is dead, and His spirit has died out—died out even in those who call Him their Redeemer! The fools! Through himself alone can man be redeemed—through himself and in himself. . . ."

He ceased, and Moses was silent also.

The two men sat side by side for some time without speaking, each busied with his own thoughts.

At length Moses asked : "And what do you want with the child?"

"I want to be her teacher," replied Schlome, "for I have learned to love her dearly in the few interviews I dared to have with her. And believe me— she is no common child! Oh, had she only been a boy! I have often thought; and then, again, I have been thankful she was a girl—you can guess why, perhaps. She has a real hunger for knowledge, and a strange longing for the light of truth. . . ."

Here the other interrupted him impatiently. "You are dreaming, Schlome! . . . Esther is scarcely nine years old, and I, her own father, have noticed nothing of the kind in her."

"Because you wouldn't see it," was the answer; "because you wouldn't see it, or, forgive me, couldn't see it. You look upon it as dreaming or folly, or else think it childish. But I know what it is for a young heart to have to bear that longing alone. Believe me, it would be a sin to let it die out for want of food. I therefore beg of you to allow me to be Esther's teacher!"

There was another long silence between the men.

At length Moses answered : "I can not, brother, and I dare not if I would. It isn't because of you that I say this—I believe that you are good, and that you would only teach the child what is good. But it would not be suitable for my daughter. I wish her to remain a simple Jewish girl; I wish it, and it must be so. Why should she learn what may make her sad, and discontented with her lot? My daughter is to grow up a pious, simple-minded woman.; it is best for her that it should be so, and that is my reason for refusing your request. I have already arranged that she should marry a rich and honorable man."

"Yes," said the Meschumed, and, for the first time during this conversation, his voice sounded bitter and hard—"yes, you are rich and have the right to do as you will: you have therefore arranged that you should have a rich son-in-law. The girl is now nine years old; in six or seven years' time you will give her to the wealthiest and most pious youth in the district, or perhaps to a widower who is even richer and more pious. She will not know him, but what of that? she will have plenty of time to make his acquaintance after marriage! Then she will probably fear him, or hate him, or else he will be indifferent to her. But what of that? What does a Jewish woman want with love? What more does she need but to love God, and her children, and—let me not forget to mention it—her little possessions? . . ."

"I don't understand you," said Moses, hesitating and astonished.

"You do not understand me!" cried the other,

springing up excitedly. "Can *you* say that—*you?*
O Moses, think of my sister. . . ."

Moses Freudenthal started like a wild creature
shot to the heart. He wanted to answer angrily, to
order Schlome to leave him at once and for ever ;
but he could not do it. His eyes involuntarily sank
before those of the despised Meschumed : after a long
and hard struggle with himself he felt constrained to
answer low and sadly, "It was not my fault."

"No," replied the other, gently ; "no, it was not ·
your fault ; it was that of your father and mine. But
remember that you, and you only, will be responsible
for what you do with your child."

He paused a while, and then finding that Moses
was too deeply moved to be able to answer, went on :
"Do not harden your heart, lest you be tempted to
evil. Remember what is written, 'Give to the thirsty
to drink.' Brother, will you allow me to show your
child the light and life for which her whole nature
thirsts ? "

Moses was unable to answer, but next day a strange
rumor was afloat in the Ghetto, to the effect that
Moses Freudenthal had become reconciled to Schlome,
the Meschumed, and had permitted him to teach his
only child ! . . .

It is of that hour that the lonely old man in the
synagogue is thinking, and it is that hour which he
curses from the bottom of his soul. The remem-

brance of it follows him as he rises with the rest of
the congregation and goes out into the spring night.
The narrow streets are full of life; the houses are
lighted up; the children and young girls are standing in the doorway of their homes waiting for the
return of their parents. The unhappy man tortures
himself as he walks with the thought of how different everything would be if he were now going home
with his son-in-law and his daughter, to be greeted
by his grandchildren at the gate. Every child's laugh,
every word of welcome that he hears, cuts him to the
heart. Ah, well! Perhaps he is not so very much
to blame when he mutters below his breath, "If God
is just, he will punish him who gained the heart of
my child only to lead her astray, and him also who
opened her ears to the words of the tempter! . . ."

At this moment he feels a hand laid upon his
shoulder, and, turning round to see who it is, starts
back as though he saw a ghost. His breath comes
thick and fast, his eyes flash, and he clinches his fist.
The man he has just cursed stands before him—a
sickly, broken old man—Schlome, the Meschumed.

"I must speak to you," he says to Moses. "I
have a letter. . . ."

"Silence, wretch!" cries the other, half mad with
rage and misery. "Silence . . . . I will not listen
. . . . May you words choke . . . ."

A crowd collects round the two men.

The Meschumed advances a few steps nearer his brother-in-law, and repeats : " I must speak to you. Curse me if you like, but listen to me. She is . . . ."

Before he can utter another word, Moses has turned and rushed away. He flies like a hunted creature through the narrow streets, across the market-place, and up to his own house. There he sinks half faint-ing on the stone seat by the door. He sits still, wait-ing till his breathing becomes more regular, and his pulses beat less quickly. Then all at once he thinks he hears some one mention his name. The first-floor windows are lighted up and widely opened ; loud laughter can be heard within the room. Frau Kasi-mira Lozinska is having an " at home" this evening. Now he hears it again quite distinctly : his name, and then a burst of laughter. He pays no attention to it, but goes into his parlor and sits down, silently pushing away the food and drink the old housekeeper sets be-fore him. " She is dead ! "—these words seem to ring in his ears and heart—"of course—she is dead ! "

Thus he sits alone in the brilliantly lighted room in a tumult of wild thoughts, of passionate internal conflict. All around him is hushed ; the melancholy sputtering of the numerous candles is the only sound to be heard.

.   .   .   .

The wife of the district judge has an " at home" to-night.

The gentlemen are in the ante-room playing at whist and *tarok*, and perhaps a little innocent game of hazard. The ladies in the drawing-room are seated round a large tea-table, drinking tea out of enormous cups, eating sweet cakes of all kinds, and talking a great deal. The only person at all out of humor is the fat wife of the fat estate agent. She is accustomed to be the principal lady in Barnow, but is dethroned for to-day by the wife of a beggarly Government official—i. e., the new registrar. For Frau Emilie comes from Lemberg, the capital of the province, and has brought with her not only the latest fashions in dress, but also a number of piquant stories. In return for these, she is of course told all the scandals of Barnow that relate to any lady who happens not to be present at the time. But that amusement soon comes to an end, as almost every one of any standing is at Frau Kasimira's this evening. Then, as luck will have it, Frau Emilie asks to be told the curious story her husband has heard about from the district judge that day.

"I can tell you that story better than any one else," answers her hostess, eagerly. "We have lived in this house for the last twelve years, and I know everything that happened. It is very interesting, for a handsome hussar is the hero of the tale. I'm sure that you can not have heard anything like it in Lemberg."

She then goes on to relate as follows:

"Well, as you know already, the story is about Esterka, the daughter of the Jew to whom this house belongs. She was ten years old when we came here, and tall of her age, with black hair and large blue eyes. She was scarcely ever to be seen, and never to be heard: she used to sit over her books all day long, and often far into the night. My daughter Malvina, who was about the same age, used to ask her to come and play with her; but the proud little Jewish girl wouldn't accept any of her invitations, she was so taken up with her reading. It was very foolish of her, and her uncle Grünstein was at the bottom of it all. Old Grünstein is a very queer sort of man—most disagreeable to have anything to do with, I should say: he's neither Jew nor Christian—quite an infidel, in fact; indeed, some people go so far as to say that he can raise the dead when he likes. Yes, I mean what I say! He can raise the very dead from their graves! And he was Esterka's teacher. He must have given her a nice sort of education, for at the end of three years she was every bit as foolish and godless as himself. To give you an example of this, let me tell you what happened one very hot August afternoon when she was with us. You must know that she embroidered beautifully, so we had asked her to come and help Malvina to finish a bit of work. As we sat at our sewing the clouds began to come up thick and fast, and soon afterward

there was a terrible storm; it thundered, lightened,
and hailed with the greatest possible fury. My daughter, who, thank God, had received the education of a
good Catholic, began to pray aloud; but the Jewess
remained calm and cool. 'Esther,' I said, 'aren't you
afraid of the judgment of God?'—'A thunder-storm
isn't a judgment of God,' answered the conceited little
thing.—'Well, then, what do you call the lightning?'
I asked.—'A discharge of atmospheric electricity,' was
her reply.—'Aren't you afraid of the lightning, then?'
—'Oh, yes,' she answered, 'because we haven't a light-
ning-conductor on the house!'—I couldn't possibly
allow such godless sentiments to pass unreproved, as
Malvina was there, so I said very sternly: 'You're a
little infidel, child; remember this, the good God
guides every flash of lightning!'—'How can that be?'
answered Miss Impudence. 'The poor peddler, Be-
risch Katz, was killed by lightning last year, when he
was crossing the open fields, although he was a very
good man; and now that he is dead, his children
haven't enough to eat.'—I said nothing more at the
time, but next day, when I happened to see old Moses,
I told him the whole story. 'The child is having a
nice sort of education,' I said in conclusion, 'and if this
kind of thing goes on, who knows what the end of it
will be?'—'It shall not go on,' he replied; 'I had made
up my mind to put a stop to it before, and what you
tell me determines me to do so at once.'—He was as

good as his word, and took away all of Esther's books.
Then he put her in the shop, and made her weigh the
sugar and sell the groceries. As for Schlome, he
turned him out of the house.

"All this took place nine years ago last summer.
One Sabbath afternoon in the following autumn Esther
came to my daughter and entreated her with tears to
lend her a German book, or else she would die. She
said that her father had taken away every one of her
books, and looked after her so strictly that she couldn't
herself get any to take their place. He did not, however, go so far as to prevent her visiting us. Our acquaintance was an honor to the girl, and besides that,
he knew that I was a woman of principle. Well, as I
said before, Esther wept and entreated in such a heart-
rending manner that I was touched. So I lent her
some German books that I happened to have in the
house: Heine's 'Reisebilder,' Klopstock's 'Messiade,'
'Kaiser Joseph,' by Louise Mühlbach, the new 'Pita-
val,' Eichendorf's poems, and the novels of Paul de
Kock. She read them all, devouring them much as a
hungry wolf does a lamb. She read them in the shop
whenever her father's back was turned, and at night
when she went to her room. The only book she didn't
like was the first novel of Paul de Kock; she brought
it back to me, and asked me to find her something else.
But I hadn't time to do so then, so I said: 'Read it,
child, read it; you'll like it when once you've fairly

begun.' I was right; she liked it so much that she never offered to give back the second novel, and after the third, she wanted to finish all by that author before reading anything else. I was able to gratify her, as we have the whole of his works. She devoured the hundred and eighty volumes in the course of one winter. For, I can assure you, these Jewish girls have no moral feeling . . . !"

The ladies all agree in regarding this statement as true. The estate - agent's wife is the only one who does not join in the chorus. For though she is very fat and rather stupid, she has a good heart.

"It wasn't right," she says very distinctly and very gravely. "You have a great deal to answer for."

The Frau Kasimira looks at her in silent astonishment. If she were not a very courteous woman, a woman of the world, and, above all, if it were not her own house, she would smile sarcastically and shrug her shoulders. As it is, she contents herself with saying apologetically, "Mon Dieu! she was only a Jewess!"

"Only a Jewess!" repeats the chorus of ladies aloud, and also in a whisper. Many of them laugh as they say . . . "only a Jewess!"

"Only a Jewess!" is echoed in a grave deep voice. The games in the ante-room are finished, and the gentlemen have rejoined the ladies unnoticed. "You have made a great mistake, madam."

It is the doctor of Barnow who speaks, a tall stately man. He is a Jew by birth. He is hated because of his religion, and feared because of his power of sarcasm. His position obliges these people to receive him into their society, and he accepts their invitations because theirs is the only society to be had in the dull little country town.

"You have made a mistake," he repeats, addressing the estate-agent's wife. "You have never been able to throw off the prejudices of your German home, where people look upon a Jew as a human being. It is very foolish of you not to have learned to look upon the subject from the Podolian point of the view !"

"Laugh as much as you like," says his hostess quickly. "I still maintain that an uneducated Jewess has very little moral feeling !"

"Yes," is the dry answer, "especially when she has been put through a course of Paul de Kock—has been given the whole of his works without exception. "But, pray, don't let me interrupt you; go on with your story."

Frau Kasimira continues :

"Very well; where did I leave off? Oh, I remember now. She had finished Kock by the spring. I had no more German books to lend her; so she begged me to subscribe to the Tarnapol lending library for her, and I at length consented to do so. I

didn't like it at all, but she entreated me to do it so
piteously, that I must have had a heart of stone to
refuse. She read every one of the books in the library, beginning with About and ending with Zschokke.
Her father had no suspicion of the truth, and he never
knew it. She used only to read in the night when
she went to her bedroom. The exertion did not hurt
her eyes at all. She had most beautiful eyes, large
and blue—blue as the sky. As to her figure, it was
queenly, slender, upright, and rounded. In short, she
was lovely—very lovely. But at the same time she
was a silly romantic. girl, who thought that real life
was like the novels she used to devour. When she
was sixteen her father told her that he wished her to
marry a son of Moschko Fränkel from Chorostko, a
handsome Jewish lad of about her own age. She said
she would rather die than marry him. But old Freudenthal isn't a man to jest with. The betrothal took
place, and beautiful Esther sat at the feast pale and
trembling as though she were about to die. I had
gone down-stairs to see the ceremony from curiosity.
My heart is not a very soft one, but when I saw
Esther looking so miserable, I really felt for the girl.
'Why are you forcing your daughter to marry against
her will?' I asked the old man. He answered me
abruptly, almost rudely, I thought : 'Pardon me ; you
don't understand ; our ways are different from your
ways. We don't look upon the chicken as wiser than

the hen. And, thank God, we know nothing of love and of all that kind of nonsense. We consider that two things are alone requisite when arranging a marriage, and these are health and wealth. The bride and bride-groom in this case possess both. I've given in to Esther so far as to consent that the marriage should be put off for a year. That will give her time to learn to do her duty. Many changes take place in a year.'

"The old man was right. Many changes take place in a year. The greatest possible change had taken place in beautiful Esterka, but it was not the change that her father had expected or wished to see. Look here, the doctor there looks upon me as hating all Jews, but I am perfectly just to them, and I tell you that the girl, although inwardly depraved, had hitherto conducted herself in the most praiseworthy manner. And yet her temptations must have been very great. She was known throughout the whole district, and every one called her the 'beautiful Jew-ess.' The inn and bar down-stairs had more visitors than Moses cared for. When the young nobles of the district came to Barnow on magisterial business, they spread out the work they had to do over three days, instead of contenting themselves with one as before ; the unmarried lawyers and custom-house offi-cials spent their whole time at the bar ; and as for the hussar officers, they took up their quarters there altogether. These men, one and all, paid their court to Esther, but she never wasted a thought upon one of them. Her father kept her as much as possible out of the way of his customers. When she met them, she returned their greeting courteously, but was as if deaf to their compliments and flattery. And if any one was rude to her, she was quite able to defend herself. Young Baron Starsky found that out to his cost—you know him, don't you? A tall fair man, and the hero of that queer story about Gräfin Jadwiga Bortynska. Well, he once met Esther as he was leaving the bar-parlor rather the worse for wine. He will never forget that meeting, because of the tremendous box on the ear that she gave him.

"There was a change in her after her engagement. Not that she was on more friendly terms with these men than before, but that she no longer rebuffed one of their number. This favored individual was a captain in the Würtemberg Hussars, Graf Géza Szapany by name. He was like a hero of romance : tall, slight, and interesting-looking, with dark hair, black eyes, and a lovely little mustache. This is no flattering portrait, I can assure you ; our friend Hortensia will bear witness that I do not exaggerate, she used to know him too. . . ."

Frau Hortensia, a handsome blonde, and wife of the assistant judge of the district, blushes scarlet, and casts an angry look at her "friend" and hostess, but forces herself to answer indifferently, "Ah yes, to be sure, I remember him. . . . He was a good-looking man."

"Good-looking," repeats Frau Kasimira. "He was more than that. He was very handsome; and *so* interesting! His manners were perfect. He thoroughly understood the art of making himself agreeable to women; but that was natural enough, for he had had plenty of experience. Beautiful Esterka was soon caught in his toils. He approached her almost shyly, and spoke to her with the utmost respect; and more than all, he paid her no compliments. That helped on his cause wonderfully. And then you mustn't forget what I told you before, that she was depraved at heart, and foolishly romantic. The affair ran the usual course. At first a few meetings, then many; at first but a few words were exchanged, afterward many; at first one kiss, then many more. . . . It was very amusing!"

Every one present seems to regard it in the same light as Frau Kasimira. The ladies giggle and the gentleman laugh. One lady alone remains grave—and she is the fat, kind-hearted German woman sitting in the corner of the sofa.

"You don't seem to be amused by the story," observes the doctor, who is sitting beside her.

"No," she answers. "It is a very sad story. The poor girl was a victim."

"Yes," says the doctor, his voice sounding deep

and low with suppressed feeling, "she was a victim.
But she was not a victim of the handsome hussar,
nor even of our kind hostess here. The cause of her
ruin lies deeper, much deeper than that. As the twilight is more eerie than complete darkness, so a half
education is more dangerous than absolute ignorance.
Darkness and ignorance alike lay a bandage over the
eyes and prevent the feet from straying beyond the
threshold of the known; knowledge and light open
the eyes of man and enable him to advance boldly on
the path that lies before him; while half knowledge
and twilight only remove part of the bandage and
leave him to grope about blindly, perhaps even cause
him to fall! Poor child! she was snatched away
from the pure stream, and her thirst was so great
that she strove to slake it in any puddles she passed
on the way. Poor child! She . . ."

Here a yawn interrupts the speaker. The fat
woman is thoroughly good and kind, but she is by
no means intellectual, and hates having to listen to
what she does not understand.

Meanwhile Frau Kasimira continues as follows:

"So Graf Géza soon succeeded in gaining complete influence over her. And when he left this to
be stationed at Marburg, she followed him there.
One Friday evening—just like to-day—when Moses
came home, he found the nest empty. There was a
great uproar down-stairs. They called her, sought

her everywhere with tears — no words can describe
the scene.   My husband went down-stairs — Moses
raged like a madman.   It all happened five years
ago, but I shall never forget that night. . . .

"The next few days were very uncomfortable and
queer.   They all went on as if Esther were dead.
The shop and bar were both closed ; the pictures were
hung with black ; the mirrors were turned with their
faces to the wall.   A small lamp was burnt in a
corner of her room for seven days and seven nights,
and during the whole of that time Moses sat on the
floor of the room barefoot and with his clothes torn.
I don't know whether it is true, but I heard that the
Jews took an empty coffin to the cemetery on the
Sunday following, and then filled in an empty grave.
I have been told that they even went so far as to
put up a gravestone to Esther !   On the eighth day
Moses rose up and went quietly about his business
again.   These Jews are such strange creatures !   Only
fancy ! he came to us that very day to ask for his
rent.   I scarcely recognized him—his hair had turned
quite gray in the course of a week.   His manner was
quiet and composed, and he seems to have forgotten
all about his daughter now.   But as everybody knows,
the Jews are fonder of their money than of their
children ! "

"Has no one heard anything more about Esther ? "
asks the fat woman.

"Yes—once. But what we heard wasn't much to be relied on. Little Lieutenant Szilagy—you remember what fibs he used to tell—went to spend his leave in Hungary on one occasion, and when he came back, he declared that he had seen Graf Géza and Esther in a box in the National Theatre at Pesth. But the little man tells so many lies that one never knows how much to believe. It may quite well have been some other pretty girl."

"Do you know," says Frau Emilie, the highly educated lady from Lemberg, "do you know what this story reminds me of? Of a very amusing play I once saw acted in Lemberg. It was translated from the English of a certain . . . oh dear! these English names . . ."

"Perhaps you mean Shakespeare?" inquires the doctor, coming to the rescue.

"Shakespeare," repeats the district judge; "he's a rather well-known poet."

Yes; a very talented man!" says the doctor, with the utmost gravity.

"You're right—Shakespeare!" continues Frau Emilie; "and the play was called 'The Merchant of Venice.' There is a Jew in it, Shylock by name, whose daughter also ran away, and who, like Moses, was far fonder of his money than of his child. I therefore propose that we should no longer call the Freudenthal of to-day by his own name, but instead of that"

—the speaker makes a long pause—"the Shylock—of Barnow!"

The registrar feels very proud of his clever wife. The gentlemen laugh, the ladies titter, and even the estate-agent's fat wife smiles as they one and all repeat:

"Ha! ha! ha! The Shylock of Barnow!"

.   .   .   .

But they do not laugh next morning. They never laugh at Shylock again—neither they nor any one else.

The wan pale light of the Sabbath morning dawns upon a woful sight. It is a damp, misty, disagreeable morning. The wind, which had risen at midnight, and had driven the heavy black clouds across the sky, covering the moon as though with a pall, has fallen; but the clouds are heavier and blacker than ever, and a thick cold mist inwraps the whole plain and the gloomy little town.

All sleep soundly in the small houses of the Ghetto. Not a step is to be heard in the narrow streets. The dogs in the courtyards, and the nightwatchman in front of the town-hall, are alone awake. The latter is usually asleep at this hour, but the dogs are making too much noise to allow him even to fall into a doze. They are barking furiously. The dogs at the town-gate are the first to begin it, then the watch-dog at the monastery takes up the chorus, and

lastly, Moses Freudenthal's black "Britan" joins in
the uproar. The wise watchman therefore makes up
his mind that some stranger is passing the monastery
and going toward the Jew's house. But it never
occurs to him to go and see who it is. The mist
makes the morning very dark, and the streets very
slippery. So the guardian of Barnow remains quietly
in his little box in front of the town-hall. "Britan
is barking so loud," he says to himself, consolingly,
"that the Jew can't help hearing him."

He is not mistaken. The people in Freudenthal's
house hear the furious barking. The old housekeeper
gets up to see what is the matter, and to call the man-
servant. As she passes her master's room, she notices
a light under the door, and, on hearing the sound of
her footsteps, old Moses comes out. He is still dressed;
he has evidently not yet gone to bed, although it is
nearly two o'clock in the morning. He looks thoroughly worn-out.

"Go back to bed," he says to the old woman; "I
will go myself and see if anything is wrong."

At the same moment the dog again barks furiously,
and then all at once begins to whine and utter short
barks of joy. They hear the huge creature jumping
about and scratching at the outer door. He has evidently recognized the person who has come up to the
house, and is trying to get to him.

The old man turns as pale as death. "Who can it

4

be?" he murmurs. Then he proceeds with tottering steps toward the entrance-hall. The housekeeper prepares to follow him, but he exclaims "Go away" so passionately, that she draws back. He takes no candle with him, for it is the Sabbath; so he feels his way to the house-door.

The old woman stands and listens. She hears the dog spring forward to meet his master, and then run with joyous whines toward the outer door.

Then she hears Moses ask, "Who is there?"

All is still. The dog alone utters a short bark.

Moses repeats his question.

An answer comes from without. The housekeeper can not hear what it is. It sounds to her like a cry of pain.

But the old man must have understood. He opens the heavy outer door, steps out, and shuts it behind him. The dog has apparently slipped out at the same time as his master, for the housekeeper can hear the stifled sound of his bark.

Then Moses's voice becomes audible; he speaks very loudly and passionately. What he says sounds at first like scolding, and then like a solemn curse or conjuration. But the old woman can not hear the words. . . . No mortal ear hears the words that Moses Freudenthal addresses to the person who had knocked at his door that dismal night.

After a minute of suspense, the housekeeper hears

the outer door creak. Moses is coming back. He returns alone. The dog has remained outside.

There is a moment's silence ; and then the house-keeper hears a heavy fall.

She seizes the candle—what does she care in her terror about the old pious custom?—and hastens to the door. There lies Moses Freudenthal, motionless and pale as death. She raises his head ; he breathes stertorously.

On perceiving this, the old woman utters a loud shriek. The man-servant and shopman, wakened by her cry, hasten to the spot. They lifted their master, and, carrying him to his room, put him to bed. Then one of them goes for the doctor of the district, who lives close by on the first floor. He bleeds the sick man, but shakes his head as he does so. The old man has had a stroke.

The housekeeper weeps, the men stand about the room awkwardly, not knowing whether to go or stay, and the doctor attends to his patient.

Thus the hours pass slowly, and the morning comes. No one remembers the stranger who had knocked at the door in the night.

Early in the morning a loud knocking is heard at the door. The night-watchman stands without, accompanied by several people who have come in early to the market. They have found a poorly-dressed, half-starved-looking young woman lying dead at the door.

Black Britan is lying beside the corpse, whining, and licking its hands. When any one tries to approach, he growls and shows his teeth.

The doctor goes on and bends over the dead woman. He lays his hand on her heart; it has ceased to beat. He then looks at the pale, worn face, and recognizes it at once.

He rises sadly, and orders the corpse to be taken to the dead-house. He then returns to the sick man, who still lies senseless.

Next day they bury Esther Freudenthal. No one knows what her religion had been—whether she had remained a Jewess, or had become a Christian. Not even her uncle Schlome, who cowers down by her bier in a stupor of grief. So they bury her where suicides are laid; and yet she had died of starvation.

A packet of letters is found in her pocket. They are all written in the same hand, and bear the same superscription—Géza. The last of these letters, which is stamped with the post-mark of a small Hungarian town, contains the following lines: "I tell you honestly that I am tired of the whole thing. I am now with my regiment, and advise you not to attempt to follow me. My sergeant, Koloman, has promised to marry you. He likes you. If you don't like him, you had better go home."

She did go home.

Old Moses does not die in consequence of the oc-

currences of that night. He lives on for a long time ;
he outlives his brother-in-law, and many happy people. He lives a gloomy, solitary, mysterious life.
When he dies, the only people who weep for him are
the mourning - women who have been hired for the
purpose. He leaves his great fortune to the wonder-
working Rabbi of Sadagóra, the most jealous oppo-
nent of light, the most fanatical supporter of the old
dark faith.

This is the story of Moses Freudenthal, whom
they called the "Shylock of Barnow."

CHANE.

(1873.)

CHANE.

MANY years have passed since poor Esther Freudenthal died at her father's feet. Moses has also been dead for a long time. The large white house opposite the Dominican monastery, which now belongs to the Rabbi of Sadagóra, looks quite as grand and well cared for as when it was owned by the stern, unhappy old man. An oval plate now hangs above the door, on which a black eagle is painted on a yellow shield, and round the edge are the words, "Royal and Imperial District Court." Petty thieves, Polish rebels, and Jewish usurers are brought to trial where Moses and his daughter had lived and suffered. These public offices occupy the ground-floor on the right of the entrance-door. The shop formerly kept by old Moses still remains on the left hand, but another name is now painted above the door—"Nathan Silberstein, Grocer and Wine-Merchant." Two words of the inscription were wrongly spelt; but that was the fault of humpbacked little Janko, who painted the sign.

The new owner has made no changes on the first floor, which is still let to the doctor and district judge. The district judge is, however, different from the one Moses Freudenthal knew. Herr Julko von Negrusz has succeeded Herr Hippolyt Lozinski, with the yellow face and attenuated figure. He differs from his predecessor in every respect. Herr Lozinski considered the Jews his prey, rich and poor alike ; and what he extorted from them he gave to poor Christians—such as the nobles, officials, and officers. His wife, Kasimira, who came of the noble family of Cybulski—which name in English means Onion—was celebrated for five German miles around Barnow for three peculiarities—her debts, her brilliant toilets, and her love of dancing. She deceived her husband so openly, that people wondered how he could continue to cock his hat so jauntily on his long yellow head.

But all this is changed.

Herr von Negrusz extorts nothing from the Jews, nor does he give great feasts to the Christians. He lives entirely in his office, and for his lovely young wife and two pretty boys. His wife is very beautiful. Her figure is straight and slender, and though her carriage is proud, she is extremely graceful. Her features are finely cut, and her dreamy dark eyes are unfathomably deep. But her most striking beauty is her rich olive complexion. Her appearance conjures up Zuleima and Zuleika, and the enchanted beauties of the East ; but it must be observed that the district judge's wife wears a cross upon a chain round her throat, and that she has printed upon her calling-cards, "Christine von Negrusz."

Strange to say, these cards form her sole connection with other people. She has no visitors, and she visits no one. Between her and the world of Barnow there is a limit of acquaintance, past which neither she nor they try to step.

If some public functionary sent to Barnow happens to be a married man, he is carefully instructed by his colleagues to borrow the old carriage and horses of old Herr von Wolanski, and drive with his wife to the large white house. Arrived there, he is to send in cards, and is warned that the customary answer received on such occasions is, that the district judge is not at home, and that *gnädige Frau* is not well. In the course of a week Herr von Negrusz and his wife drive in the same carriage to return the visit, and the ceremony is acted over again with the parts reversed. All intercourse then ceases beteen the two families. This custom is invariable.

Another curious circumstance is, that Frau von Negrusz never goes out of the house alone. Once or twice a week she takes a walk with her husband. The inhabitants of Barnow are accustomed to walk in the new park surrounding the castle of Gräfin Jadwiga Bortynska, *née* Polanska. Unlike other people, the

district judge and his wife always take their constitu-
tional in the deserted garden by the river-side, and
close to the old castle. The direct road to these pleasure-grounds is through the Jews' quarter; but this unsociable pair avoid the nearest way, and choose rather
to go all round the outskirts of the town. One might
have supposed their reason to have been that they
wished to escape the dust and bad odors of the Ghetto;
but this hardly accounts for it, as when once caught in
a storm, they made the same long round in the pouring
rain.

Herr von Negrusz looks everybody pluckily in the
face, and never avoids meeting his friends; why should
his wife be so unsociable, and what proscription separates her from the rest of the world?

You have only to ask the gossip and newsmonger
of Barnow—the magnificent Frau Emilie, wife of the
new registrar. Her husband has lived ten years in
Barnow, but he is still called the "new registrar," to
distinguish him from his colleague, who has been there
twice as long. Frau Emilie will show you a calling-
card, and answer as follows: "How can one associate
with such a person? Look at her card—why has she
not had it printed in the proper way, with her maiden
name in the usual place? Because it would not look
well to put 'Christine von Negrusz, *née* Bilkes, *di-
vorcée* Silberstein.' Her real name is Chane, her father
is Nathan Bilkes, and another Nathan—Nathan Silber-

stein—is her first husband. Negrusz is eccentric. First
he wanted to marry the daughter of a millionaire, an
Armenian baron, and when this was forbidden, he suddenly comforted himself by falling in love with the
rather good-looking Jewess, and he bought her from
her husband. . . ."

"Bought?" you will ask with surprise — "for
money—for hard cash?"

"Of course—why not?" your informant will reply.
"Are you really surprised? To a Jew everything is
salable—even a wife. It is said that Negrusz had to
pay down a thousand gulden. If you do not believe
me, ask every one in Barnow, or, better still, ask Nathan Silberstein how much he got. He is a wine-merchant, and though he is continually traveling about, he
is sure to be at home for the great feasts. He will tell
you that he gave her up to the district judge willingly.
Now, I ask you, can we associate with such a woman?"

Emilie, the magnificent, is right for the most part.
Frau Christine was really Chane, and she had been
Chane Bilkes, and afterward Chane Silberstein. The
wine-merchant had given her up voluntarily to the district judge. She was right also when she said that it
was impossible for her—Emilie—to know such a person.
She was quite wrong about the money transaction.

The price paid was not a bank-note, but a human
heart.

.   .   .   .

The synagogue is a gray weather-beaten building, erected long ago, almost in the middle ages. The country people call it the Judenburg (Jews' strong-hold), because the Jews once took refuge in it, and intrenched themselves there, when Prince Czartoryski came to murder and rob them. One of his reasons for doing so was that he wanted sport, and there were no foxes or wild boars to be found in the neighborhood in the hunting season; and another was, that he wanted money. The Jews hid themselves and their property behind the walls and iron bars of the syna-gogue, and held out until the men of Jagiellnica arrived from their neighboring fortress, and relieved them. At that time the walls of the Judenburg were strong, and the iron-work firm; but the bars are all broken now, or they are lost, and the walls are half in ruins. As if to testify to the importance of the building as a holy refuge, the poorest of the Jews' houses are built round it on three sides. On the fourth side, the sluggish river Lered flows so close to the synagogue that there is only space for two dwell-ings. One of these is a large new house, painted yellow—an unusual decoration in this vicinity—and the other is a dirty, ruinous cottage clinging forlornly to the bank of the river. The yellow house seems to be shoving its poorer neighbor over the brink, the moldering walls of the hovel hang so directly above the slow sad water. The rich wine-merchant, Manasse Silberstein, used to live with his son in the large house, and a very poor man, Nathan Bilkes, had lived for many years in the hovel.

Nathan had been a *dorfgeher* (peddler) as long as his strength had lasted, and then he spent a weak lonely old age upon his hardly earned savings, eked out by the charity of the community. He had become prematurely old and weak, like most people of his hard-working, poverty-stricken class.

A *dorfgeher* means, in the language of his co-religionists, a traveler who gains his livelihood by supplying the surrounding villages with the necessaries of life. On Sundays he tramps out of the town with an enormous pack upon his back, in which is stored all that the heart of a Ruthenian peasant could wish for, except the one thing most desired—for the *dorfgeher* does not sell schnapps.

Everything else he sells : straw hats, leather belts, boots, clasp-knives, flowers, ribbons, corals, love-philters, stuffs for gowns, spindles, linen, tallow, hardware, images of the saints, charms, wax-candles, needles, linen thread, and newspapers of the last week. He sells everything, and all are his customers —from the cavalry officers, who buy his smuggled cigars, and the pastors and gentry, who buy his fine stuffs, to the poorest peasant. Throughout the whole week he goes from village to village, from house to house—in the height of summer and the depth of winter. He knows everybody, and all know him. If they require his wares they invite him to cross their thresholds; if they want to buy nothing they drive him away, and if he does not go immediately they hound their dogs at him. The peasant and the noble, the chaplain and the young lieutenants, sharpen their wits at his expense; and if their jokes are not always ready, they try their switches and spurs. But he never wearies, and from early morning until late evening he raises his hoarse cry, and haggles and cheats wherever he can. If he can not get money in exchange for his wares, he will take what he can get—skins, grain, chickens, ducks, or eggs. On Friday afternoons he returns to town, and for one whole day he feels himself a man; but on Sunday he becomes nothing but a *dorfgeher* again. . . .

Nathan Bilkes was a *dorfgeher*, and the above is a description of his life, which differed in no way from that of others of his trade. His father had found him a wife in due time. She had proved most excellent, but had died soon after her marriage, leaving two children.

The children grew up, strong and beautiful, in the dark cheerless cottage, as one sometimes sees sweet flowers blooming in the midst of rubbish and decay. But their father bewailed their strength and beauty, for these qualities lost them to him. His children so passed out of his life that he grew to look upon them as dead. The son was obliged to become a soldier, because Nathan could not pay the fifty gulden that were required to obtain his release. Bär Blitzer, the broker, had said that it could be done for fifty gulden, but the money was not there. The lad went to Italy with his regiment, and after the battle of Magenta his name was in the official list as "missing." His old father waited long for his return, but he never came back. His daughter, too, died to him. "My Chane," the old man took care to say, "was a beautiful Jewess; but I do not know the heathen (*goje*) Frau Christine."

The *dorfgeher* had not foreseen that his daughter would be a source of trouble to him. His Chane had been as obedient as she was lovely, modest, and industrious. See was not alone beloved by her father—she was a universal favorite.

No one grudged her good luck when old Manasse Silberstein sought her hand in marriage for his only son Nathan. It was a great and unexpected good fortune; for these people are strictly divided into classes, and the rich and poor seldom intermarry. This custom is natural; for the only occupation they were permitted to follow was money-making, thus the possession of wealth has been their sole happiness for many generations.

The poor peddler was at first incredulous. Old Manasse was very rich, and had a large grocery business, and a prosperous trade in Hungarian and Moldavian wines. It was a great distinction for the poor girl that his choice fell upon her.

Nathan Silberstein was a man of irreproachable character. He was a fine-looking young fellow, honest, straightforward, and intelligent, and knew the Talmud as well as he knew his trade. As he was to be a merchant, his father had had him taught High German. With the help of his teacher he learned reading and writing, and waded through a "complete letter-writer," and a "complete index of German municipal law." These two books were supposed to represent his German library; but hidden in his bookcase, under great Hebrew folios, was one other little German book. On Saturday afternoons, when he went to spend his holiday in the park, he took this little volume in his pocket. He read it in a solitary corner where the green leaves rustled around him, and at these times he felt something within him moving in sympathy with the poetry, of which he was unconscious during the rest of the week. Perhaps it was his heart beating. On the back of the book the title was written in gilt letters, "Schiller's Poems."

When his father told him he had chosen him a wife, and who she was to be, his heart was untouched. He answered dutifully, "As you will, father;" but the color left his face as he spoke. The girl was as obe-

dient to her father as he was to his, only she blushed
instead of turning pale when she heard the name of her
future husband.

The betrothal took place, and three months later
they were married.

In the interval, Nathan gave his *fiancée* presents of
costly pearls and precious stones ; and she embroidered
a robe in gold and silver for him to wear in the synagogue. Their conversations were always on indifferent
subjects. They did not talk of themselves or their
future life, and they did not talk of the past ; for
though they had been neighbors all their lives, they
had no mutual recollections.

The marriage was solemnized with great pomp and
ceremony : wine flowed liberally, mountains of meat
and confectionery were consumed, and the best musi-
cians and merry-andrews enlivened the guests. The
young people then took up their abode in the large
roomy house opposite the Dominican monastery, which
Manasse had prepared for his son. They led a busy
life ; their days were spent in labor, and they lived on
pleasant friendly terms with one another. They were
both good and well-disposed, and as they had never
expected their married life to be spent in an earthly
paradise, they were not disappointed. Custom, a common occupation, and mutual respect bound them to
each other. Time passed uneventfully until the end of
the first year, when a child was born, and the young

father again felt his heart beat as it had not done for a long time. The infant only survived its birth a few weeks, and grief brought the young couple into closer sympathy than before. Old Manasse died about the same time, and the whole responsibility of the business fell upon their shoulders. Nathan had to go away on long journeys, and Chane became a trustworthy stewardess of the great house. She learned to read and write German, so as to be able to help her husband in the business, while his personal comforts were her ceaseless care. He had the greatest esteem for her, and brought her many presents from Lemberg and Czernowitz. They were contented with their lot, and were happy enough.

Happy enough—why were they not quite happy?

Because they did not love one another. They knew nothing of love except that Christians, previous to marriage, fell in love; and what concern had a Jew in Christian usages?

They were happy enough, and their married life seemed firmly founded on esteem for each other, and on their common interests and work; but the storms of passion were to shake the structure to its base, and after throwing it down, were to carry them onward to grief and pain.

. . . .

Barnow is a very small town, a squalid nook in a God-forgotten corner of the earth, where the great

current of life hardly seems to cause the faintest
ripple—but it has its *casino*. This is only a modest
little room in the court behind Nathan's shop, containing two tables and a few chairs. Nathan had opened
it for the use of his principal customers. Here the
officials and magnates of Barnow are accustomed to
drink their morning glasses and discuss politics ; and
if their wives allow them, they do the same again in
the evening. The high-born Florian von Bolwinski,
a squire without land, and a bachelor, drinks not only
his morning and evening glasses in this room, but sun-
dry others also, filling up the intervals with expeditions to make love to a cook, or squeeze a Jew, or
execute some important business. The former district
judge, Herr Hippolyt Lozinski, had been a constant
customer ; and the little room did him one good service
in giving him a red nose, which was a fine contrast to
his yellow complexion. When the red deepened to
ruby color he died, rather to the delight of the district,
and to the grief of his many admirers. Frau Kasimira
retired to the estate of the Von Cybulskies, a small,
heavily mortgaged farmhouse near Tarnopol ; and the
new district judge, Herr Julko von Negrusz, took up
his residence in the first floor of the white house. He
took the place of his predecessor at the *casino* also,
but without frequenting it so continually as he had
been used to do.

Herr von Negrusz was a man of about thirty.

He was recognized at once to be an excellent jurist, and when better known, he was also considered a good fellow. A district judge in Podolia is a sort of demigod, and is either the blessing or curse of the district. Herr von Negrusz made a good use of his power. There is not much to be said about his external appearance : he was a slightly built man, with quiet brown eyes and a face that could neither be called handsome nor ugly. The custom-house officer's three sallow elderly daughters considered him a barbarian, and quite unsusceptible to the charms of women. He did not care for ladies' society.

Herr von Negrusz soon became a constant guest in the little parlor behind the grocer's shop. He went there daily when he left the office, and spent half an hour reading the newspapers before going home to the dinner prepared by his old housekeeper. As the entrance by the court was inconvenient and not very clean, he always, like most of the guests, went through the shop where Nathan Silberstein's beautiful wife superintended the business. It was his habit to pass her with a bow. He never talked and joked with her, as did most of the older men and the young officers. He had no particular reason for acting thus, except that much laughing and joking was not in his way. He may also have thought that what these men called compliments were probably objectionable to her ; but if so, he was mistaken—Chane was indifferent to what they said, and regarded their talk as one of the annoyances inseparable from attendance in the shop, as, for example, the draughts. Her manner was very decided, and she was well able to protect herself from impertinence. She answered the elder men with the same lightness as they used in speaking to her, while she greeted the officers curtly. and laconically. When love was made the subject of conversation, she would laugh and joke almost extravagantly. Love was not only an enigma to her, for she had never felt it, but it was positively ludicrous in her eyes. Whoever ventured, between the first and second pints, to say to her, "I love you," she openly derided and inwardly despised; but whoever attempted to slip his arm round her waist . . . well, to find this out, you have only to ask little Lieutenant Albert Sturm, a forward, ill-favored, saucy young fellow, why his right cheek was once redder and rounder than his left for the space of a week.

She never needed to protect herself from word or look of the district judge. For the first three months after his arrival they did not exchange a word. Such stiffness was most unusual in Barnow, where every one knew each other, more especially as she and Herr von Negrusz inhabited the same house, and Chane expressed her surprise openly and unaffectedly to her husband.

One day Nathan stood at the shop-door for a long time in earnest conversation with the district judge and Florian von Bolwinski. At last Negrusz went away to his office, while Florian entered the shop with the merchant, in order to drink an extra glass for the good of his digestion.

"Nathan," said Chane, "what a strange man the district judge is! He must be very proud! He has never yet spoken to me."

"No, he is not at all proud," answered Nathan. "He is one of the most good-natured men I know, but he is not a great talker. Why he is so silent I can not tell—perhaps he is unhappy."

"Ho, ho!" growled Florian. "What a vain woman your wife is, Pani Nathan! We are all at her feet, but that is not enough for her. She wants young Herr Julko to be the next victim. Ho, ho, ho! All her trouble will be thrown away upon him, however, for he is already in love. God's punishment is in store for her!"

Chane waited patiently until the old toper had finished speaking: she was accustomed to his rude witticisms.

"We are not all as light-hearted as you are," she answered, "and this man really seems too sensible to be capable of falling in love."

Herr Florian put his hands on his sides and laughed and sniggered. "Ho, ho!" he gasped.

"Did you ever hear such nonsense? . . . Ho, ho, ho! . . . As if only stupid people could fall in love! . . . Am I stupid? and—Pani Nathan, are you not jealous?—I am in love with her. To punish you, I must assure you that he is already disposed of! . . . his heart is buried in a grave. Ho, ho, ho!"

"Fool!" muttered Chane impatiently, while Herr Florian staggered into the *casino* with Nathan.

She could not get what he had told her out of her head, and in the evening, when she sat arranging business letters with her husband, who was to leave home next day, she suddenly asked—

"What did Bolwinski mean by saying that Herr von Negrusz's heart was buried in a grave?"

"I do not know," replied Nathan; "but the story goes that he was in love with a girl who died, and that he will never marry. It may be true, for Christians are fools when they are in love."

"Ah!" said Chane, staring thoughtfully at the flame of the lamp.

She soon took her pen again, and finished a letter to Moses Rosenzweig, ordering a barrel of herrings and five hundredweights of sugar from Czernowitz.

.   .   .   .

Next day a strange thing happened.

Herr Florian Bolwinski is not only a fat man, he is also a good-natured man. As he has never injured

5

any one, he is not afraid of any one—except his
landlady, although he has never injured her. He is
good-natured, but he has one great fault—he tells
everything that he knows, and even invents a little
now and then. These additions are the fruit, partly
of a vivid imagination, and partly of his numerous
potations. Next morning, when he sat alone in
the *casino* with the district judge, he related how
Frau Chane had opened her heart to him, and had
confessed, with torrents of tears, her mad love for
Herr von Negrusz, and that she felt inclined to kill
herself in despair, because the object of her passionate
love did not take any notice of her, and would not
waste one word upon her, even if she were dying.

Herr Florian did not make his story as short as I
have given it above, but he went into every little
particular, giving the most graphic descriptions of the
whole scene.

He interrupted himself several times to laugh,
"Ho, ho, ho!" and ejaculate, "Do you see!" He
had to do this to give himself breath, for Herr von
Negrusz said not a word. He listened gravely, only
occasionally allowing a sarcastic smile to play upon
his lips. Herr Florian disliked this smile, and as
often as he saw it he could not help feeling embarrassed. This he tried to hide by adorning his tale
still more. "Now what do you think of it all?"
he concluded, out of breath.

"What do I think of it?" repeated the district judge. "I only admire your wonderful imagination. Adam Mickiewicz is nothing to you."

"What! what!—ho, ho! you do not believe me! My dear Herr von Negrusz, I do not deserve this. Have you ever heard me tell a lie? And besides that, what good would it do me? No; on my honor, I am speaking the truth. I was quite sorry for the poor woman. She is over head and ears in love with you. I never saw anything like it—even I, who know women so well. Over head and ears, over head and ears; and now I want to know what I am to say to her? Nathan is away—do you understand?—away for three weeks—ho, ho! The woman . . ."

"Herr von Bolwinski," interrupted the district judge, rising and folding up the newspapers, which he had been glancing through, "you, who are a Catholic nobleman, think you may say what you like of the wife of the Jew Silberstein behind her back. I must, however, tell you that if I did not know that the story you have just told me is a lie from the first word to the last. . . ."

"Herr von Negrusz! . . ."

"I repeat it—a lie from the first word to the last. Had you really been the bearer of a message of love to me from a faithless woman, I should have declined any further acquaintance with you. You have been

joking in your peculiar way, which is certainly not
my way, for I object to jokes at the expense of such
worthy people as this Jewish couple. I recommend
you not to continue such jokes when you find any of
your butts as reluctant as I . . ."

Herr Florian lost his temper completely. His
story was not credited, and his good joke was lost.
This he might have pardoned, as he was accustomed
to the incredulity of his hearers, but Herr von Negrusz took his story seriously, almost tragically. He
treated him like a schoolboy, and that he could not
stand. He felt that his honor would not allow him
to retract his words, so he rose, and with much ges-
ticulation, said in an overbearing way—

"Do you know to whom you are speaking—do
you hear? Do you know to whom you are speaking,
I ask? You are speaking to me, Florian von Bolwinski. You must respect what I say ; remember
what is due to me. I never heard such language.
A liar and a go-between, am I? . . . ho, ho! I
must be respected. Remain virtuous if you choose,
but what I tell you is true. Chane is in love with
you—madly in love . . ."

"Be silent !"

These words, spoken in a sharp incisive voice, interrupted his flow of words. He looked toward the door,
and his arms fell to his sides, the blood forsaking his
cheeks. Herr von Negrusz turned crimson.

"Be silent," repeated Chane, stretching her hand toward the fat, trembling little man. Drawn up to her full height, she stood in the doorway, looking as proud and beautiful as a queen.

Herr Florian let his head sink and his under lip fall, and altogether looked very sheepish. Chane closed the door, and walked up to the two men.

"Did—you—listen?" stammered the old sinner, trying to laugh.

"I did not listen," answered Chane, emphatically. "It is not my custom to try to hear what gentlemen say in this room. It is no concern of mine. I was engaged in that part of the shop where the spices are; it is so close to the door that I could not help overhearing. It was bitter enough to do so, but it is harder still to be obliged to speak for myself." As she said this the hot blood rushed to her face. She hesitated, and then continued: "But Nathan is not at home, and I am compelled to tell you myself, to your face, Herr von Bolwinski, that you are a liar. Yesterday I did ask my husband if Herr von Negrusz was proud, as he never spoke to me, as other gentlemen do. I meant nothing wrong, and therefore, Herr von Bolwinski . . . you . . . you ought to be ashamed . . ."

Herr von Bolwinski did as he was bid; he was ashamed. His face fell, and his eyes sought the ground. Herr von Negrusz, on the contrary, fixed his eyes upon Chane. It was dangerous, even for one whose heart was "buried in the grave," to drink in her marvelous beauty.

"I thank Herr von Negrusz," continued Chane, with increasing hesitation, and blushing more deeply than before, "for showing a friendly interest in Nathan and me; and if he will not speak to me, I must speak to him, and tell him that he is rightly called a noble-minded man, and for my part, I thank him . . ."

Like Herr Florian, the district judge found no words of reply, and looked down somewhat abashed. He seized his hat, and bowing respectfully, left the room.

His old housekeeper, who had a great regard for him, was distressed at his loss of appetite that evening, for he sent away his favorite dishes almost untouched.

.   .   .   .

The days passed, and imperceptibly a bond of love was formed between these two hearts, which was sinful and criminal in the sight of God and man.

The scene in the little wine-shop had had no apparent consequences, except that Herr von Bolwinski took the rest of his potations at home that day. Of course he took an extra quantity, to console him for what he considered his undeserved rebuff. Next day he appeared as usual, passing Chane in the shop.

Herr von Negrusz also came as usual in the middle of the day. That he should do so was not a matter of surprise. It was, however, astonishing that things went on in the old way. Bolwinski continued his customary badinage, and getting no reply from Chane, he said, "Ho, ho! you are proud, but I love you all the same!" while Herr von Negrusz only bowed as before.

What was his reason?

It is not difficult for people to deceive themselves when they wish to do so. "I will not speak to her," he said to himself, "lest I should give the old gossip an opportunity for sarcasm, or the invention of fresh slanders." At the same time he was conscious that this was not his real reason, and sometimes he was childish enough to be angry with the woman whose beauty tempted his heart to be untrue to its natural sense of honor.

It was not the bashfulness of which the lively Emilie accused him; because, after she had on one occasion pressed his hand confidentially, he had not offered to shake hands with her again. Neither was it that "unsusceptibility to the charms of women" of which the three graces complained. No sensible, clever man is ever bashful, and what did his unsusceptibility amount to? Alas! the beautiful and outraged woman had made a deeper impression on his heart than was altogether pleasant to him. The

wanton conduct of Herr von Bolwinski had placed
him in such a peculiar position toward a woman with
whom he was unacquainted, that he could not hit
upon the right tone or words with which to address
her. He certainly did not feel at ease in her presence,
although he swore to himself that he was so. He
continually said to himself, "I will not speak to her,
so that that wicked· old woman in trousers may have
no reason for chatter; besides, I have nothing to
talk to her about." He knew that he was deceiving
himself, and that he was behaving badly; but as
time passed on, he found it more and more impossible to break the silence which he knew to be a mistake. He longed to know what she thought of him.

And Chane never spoke of him, even to her husband. She had talked about him openly before the
scene in the wine-room, and now she could do so no
longer. She did not even tell Nathan, on his return
home after a month's absence, of the gross conduct of
Herr von Bolwinski. "Why should I make him angry?" she thought; but she knew that she was unwilling to mention the name of Herr von Negrusz.
An inexplicable reticence prevented her from doing so.
She thought so much about him, and yet she could not
speak of him. Every day her imagination took a different turn. Sometimes she thought it was not nice of
him to treat her with such marked indifference; and at
other times she wondered if the haughty Christian

really believed she was in love with him, and wished to show her that she was nothing to him. "He need not do that," she thought, "for he is certainly nothing to me. But then he stood up for me nobly, and perhaps he does not intend to give that fat, ugly Bolwinski an opportunity for further lies. It must be true that his heart is buried in the grave. He loves a dead woman so truly that he will never speak to a living one. He does not even talk to the custom house officer's wife. How is it possible to love one who is dead—and what is love? . . ."

The Power that shapes our lives often uses strange means. Two people were being brought together who were not on speaking terms !

They maintained silence for three long months, though they saw one another daily. The summer passed away, the yellow leaves in the monastery garden began to fall ; the vintage came, and Nathan started on his long rounds through Hungary and Moldavia. He was to return on the Sabbath before the great feast. "Take care of yourself, and see that you get good vinegar out of the spoiled must," were his parting words. He embraced his wife, calmly kissing her on the brow. He little thought that he did so for the last time.

. . . .

One beautiful sunny day in September Chane was busy in the shop, and Herr von Bolwinski and the collector of taxes were talking politics in the *casino*.

Everything was as usual. Herr von Negrusz stepped into the shop. He lifted his hat, and was passing on, but was prevented by a cask of herrings, which filled the passage.

"You must come round here," said Chane, pointing behind the counter.

"Thank you," he said, passing her. Then he stopped, and added, "You are making changes here." He wished to say something, and could think of nothing better.

"Yes; for the fruit season."

"There is a splendid crop this year . . ."

"Particularly of apples . . ."

"And the wine promises well, I hear. Where is Herr Nathan just now?"

"At Hegyallja, I believe; but I do not know for certain. He has not much time for writing when he is traveling. Perhaps he is at Tokay now." Pride in the flourishing state of the business here triumphed over her shyness, and she continued: "We opened up a good trade with Potocki and Czartoryski last spring, so we now import wines direct from Tokay, as well as from the Rhine."

"I congratulate you on doing so well!" he said, lightly, and passed into the *casino.*

This was their first conversation, and Herr von Bolwinski could not have found any love-making in it, even after his thirtieth pint.

The ice was, however, broken, and many similar conversations followed, sometimes about the weather, or trade, or little everyday events. It was strange that while they were on distant terms, they were shy of one another; but on knowing each other better, they became firm friends. They might now be said to stand at cross-roads. Their simple daily intercourse might put an end to the peculiar feelings toward each other that had been produced by their first acquaintance, and subsequent coldness of manner; or it might bring about a still more dangerous juxtaposition. They were unconscious of the different paths that lay before them, and as they saw more of one another, and enjoyed the pleasure of each other's society more and more, they did not know that they had already entered upon the road which must lead to sorrow and renunciation, or to shame. . . .

Surely, had they known they would not have ventured on dangerous subjects of conversation, which gave opportunities for the expression of deep feeling and the revelation of each other's hearts. For instance, she allowed him to know that Herr von Bolwinski had told her of his love for one who had died. She almost joked about it, but was immediately sorry when she saw the gravity of his face.

"I have wounded you," she said, regretfully.

"No, no," he answered, "but I should have liked to be the first to tell you."

He then told her the simple story of his first love.

When he was a student in Munich he had fallen in love with a young girl of noble family, to whom he gave lessons. She returned his affection; but the world was too strong for them, and she married some one else, only to die after a short wedded life.

To the Jewess his story sounded like a fairy tale. A few months before, she would not have understood his feeling at all, and even now it was partly incomprehensible to her. She showed this by her next question.

"And you love her still?" she asked.

"She is dead," he replied, "and I do not love her in the same way as I loved the living woman; but her memory will be dear to me as long as I live. I shall never forget her."

Chane looked thoughtfully before her.

"Love must be strong," she whispered.

He made no reply. Perhaps he had not heard what she said.

Weeks fled rapidly, and the time of the great feast came nearer. Nathan would soon return home, and they talked of him continually, praising his industry, his honorable character, and his good honest heart. It is surprising that they should have spoken of him so often, but perhaps they did it because they felt they ought to strengthen their recollection of his existence. He was the barrier that stood between them, and respect for him was their last safeguard.

The day of Nathan's arrival dawned; it was the Friday before the Jewish new year. The decisive word was yet unspoken. The fatal time was, however, near when the scales should fall from their eyes, and they should see the abyss that yawned beneath them.

.   .   .   .

It was October. The rain had fallen ceaselessly all night, making the country and the dark little town look doubly desolate. Toward morning the wind rose and scattered the clouds, blowing down the narrow, tortuous streets, and robbing the poplars of the last red leaves that clung to their branches. It was one of those miserable days when sorrow and loneliness seem doubly heavy to those who have to bear their weight.

Chane was alone in the shop. No customers were likely to come in such weather. She watched the wind sporting with the leaves. Without any apparent reason for unhappiness, her heart felt heavy.

At last Rosel Juster came in. She was a very poor, but pretty and lively girl. She made great purchases of sugar, almonds, raisins, and spices.

"You are preparing for your betrothal," said Chane in a friendly tone. "I have heard of it, and wish you every happiness. He is a lucky man."

"Thank you," answered the girl; "the betrothal is to be on Tuesday, and the wedding will be on the second Sabbath after that. We have to think of his little children—he is a widower."

"You will have a great deal to do."

"Oh, I should think nothing of the work, but he has a sister living with him, and he is an old man; but what is the good of talking about it?"

"Then you would rather not marry him?"

Rosel looked at her in surprise. "When are we women ever consulted as to what we should like?" she asked. "I am a poor girl, and he takes me, and provides for me—that is all that I have to do with it." She shrugged her shoulders, passed her hand over her eyes, and went on quickly: "Please give me two ounces of ginger."

Chane said no more, but turned to weigh out the requisite quantity of ginger. Her hands trembled as she twisted up the little paper packet, and she made several mistakes with the weights.

"You are not well, I am sure," said Rosel, as she prepared to go. "You look so pale!"

"I am tired," answered Chane, sinking into a chair.

As the door closed behind the girl, she let her face fall between her hands, and sat a long time buried in thought. The words spoken by Rosel rang in her ears: "When are we women ever consulted as to what we should like? I am a poor girl, and he has taken me, and provided for me, that is all—my God, all! . . ."

She kept her eyes firmly closed, but she could not shut them to the truth any longer. Her whole life lay before her, and she knew that she was living a lie. "I belong to Nathan, body and soul—not because it was my will—not because it was his will —but because our fathers desired it. And now, when I feel that I am a human being, with a heart and will of my own—when I love another, I must either be miserable, or . . ."

She did not finish her sentence, for she was no longer able to control her thoughts. She was filled with self-commiseration, and burning tears fell from her eyes. She forgot where she was, and that he whom she loved, and yet feared to meet, might come at any moment. She was first roused by the monastery bell ringing at twelve o'clock, and tried to recover her composure.

It was too late. He stood within the door he had just opened.

They had never hitherto spoken of their love for each other. They had scarcely known that it existed. But when he came near her, and took her hand in his, gazing into her large, soft, tearful eyes, which were fixed pathetically upon his face, their love was revealed to him, and all the sorrow it must

bring. She, too, knew that her love was returned as
he gently smoothed her hair back from her forehead, and tried to comfort her. Then he let her
hands fall and left her side.

"We shall have much to endure," he said, as if
their love and all its consequences were mutually
understood. "But we must be firm. I have much to
say to you, but this is not the right time or place ; and
this evening"—he hesitated, and then continued :
"your husband is coming back, and I will not ask you
to give me an interview in secret from him. I will
write to you, and tell you what I think we ought
to do."

He pressed her hand and went into the *casino*.

Chane got up from her chair, and sent the appren-
tice, who had been rubbing up the silver and brass
utensils in preparation for the feast, into the shop.
She remained in the kitchen preparing for the Sabbath,
and for the return of her husband. She did everything carefully, but her manner was different from
usual.

"Have you a headache, ma'am ?" asked the maid-
servant, seeing her suddenly clasp her hands upon her
brow, as if she were trying to recollect something.
She felt confused and at a loss, but yet there was some
secret source of joy.

In the evening the office-boy brought her a note.

"From the district judge to your husband," he

said; but when she opened the envelope, she found that it contained a letter addressed to herself. She did not open it, trembling for its purport.

Dusk had fallen, and candles were brought. She repeated the beautiful old prayer dutifully, that light and peace should dwell in the house, and that God's mercy should avert every sorrow, pain, and grief. . . . She knew the few words of the formula by heart, and yet this evening they fell slowly from her lips. She doubted that she was worthy to pray to God—she a Jewess, who had in her possession a letter from her Christian lover !

Overcome with fatigue and anxiety, she sank upon a chair, and looked at the outside of the letter. It was sealed. It was a sin to break a seal upon the Sabbath. "It is not my greatest sin," she thought, as she tore open the letter.

Herr von Negrusz wrote of his love for her, and that he must die or go mad without her. "Become a Christian, and be my wife. The sin against your husband will not be so great as the sin against our love, if you refuse. I know that you love me. Only tell me that you will come to me, and all else is my care."

She crushed the letter in her hand, and threw it down. Then she picked it up, straightened it out, and reread it. Her hands fell from the table, and bending over them, her tears fell fast. She stammered convulsively : "O my God! help me, enlighten me. Let me not become like Esther Freudenthal, and end my days in shame and remorse. I have been a faithful wife. . . . I can not break my marriage vows . . . but I love him, and feel that life is worthless away from him. He is a good man . . . but were he as wicked as the hussar who ruined Esther . . . O my God! desert me not. . . ."

Crying thus in the agony of her soul, she did not hear the door open, or a man's step behind her. A hand was laid upon her shoulder. She looked up, her husband stood before her.

"Thank God!" he cried, joyfully, "I am home at last. The storm has made the roads . . ." He stopped and looked at her. . . . "Chane," he added, anxiously, "how ill you look! what is the matter?"

She did not answer, and his glance fell on the letter. He reached toward it, and she did not try to stop him. He read the first line, and became as pale as death. "To you—writing to you thus!" He read a little further, and then looked at the signature. "From him! This is a blow I did not expect." He read on. His eyes seemed starting out of their sockets, his hand trembled, and his face showed how he suffered. "What?" he cried, when he had reached a certain point. "What? Is this true?" He ceased, and she slipped on to the floor and clasped his knees, while he finished reading the letter.

He then threw it on the table, and bending over her, said sternly, "Rise and be seated."

She obeyed.

"I only wish to know one thing," he went on, standing in front of her—"the Christian writes that you love him. . . . Is it not a lie ? . . . Chane, the Christian lies ? . . ."

Lower and lower she bent her head. "Kill me," she said, "for I deserve it. What he writes is true. I do love him."

Nathan started convulsively. His usually placid features were strangely agitated. "The truth !" he hissed ; "and you remain in my house, you false wife ? "

She looked him in the face with flashing eyes.

"Nathan !" she cried, "I swear by my dead mother that he touched my hand to-day for the first time."

He gave a short laugh.

"What if I believe you ?" he said. "Shall we divide you between us ? Shall I possess you, and he have your love ? Are you not mine, body and soul ? and if you could not be altogether mine, why did you become my wife ? "

She stepped close up to him, and said, with a despairing gesture, and a sharp ring in her voice: "Do not be so hard, Nathan. I have been a true wife to you ; but when you ask why I married you, I reply, that my wishes were never consulted."

Her words seemed to strike him, for he could not answer, and there was a long silence.

She buried her face in the sofa-cushions.

At last he said, " Go—we will talk of this to-morrow."

She left the room.

He bolted the door and resumed his restless pacing up and down. The old servant knocked at the door—she had brought the supper-tray, but he dismissed her at once. She went away grumbling, and he heard her afterward saying to the cook: "God knows what is the matter! The master has locked himself into the parlor, and the mistress is in her bedroom. Neither of them will have any supper."

A hot flush of shame mounted quickly to Nathan's face.

"The servants suspect something already," he thought, " and soon all the world will wonder what has happened. Old Jutta is right; God alone knows what misery has fallen on my house, and God alone can help, for I know not what to do."

He threw himself down on the sofa, and thought it all over again, but he could not keep still, and soon started up and began to walk up and down the room again.

"How foolish it was of me to say that God alone could help!" he thought. "God can not be expected to work miracles for our individual needs. What can

God do but let him die, or me?—that would solve the difficulty."

He pressed his burning brow on the window-pane, and stared out into the darkness. "I possessed a treasure, and I did not know its value until another, who was wiser than I, came and took it from me. Perhaps—perhaps I deserve it. . . .

"Deserve it!" he repeated. "No, no, she is my wife, and whoever takes her from me is a robber and a coward. . . .

"He is a coward! . . . He, who always used to be such a good, straightforward man. I can scarcely believe that he could have been so wicked. . . . It must have been her fault—her fault alone.

"But oh, is a wife like other property, as I have always thought? Is she no more than any other chattel, such as an ornament or a house? Has she not a will like every other human being? And has that will ever been consulted? . . .

"That was the sin, and now we are suffering from its consequences.

"I was not to blame in those old days; nor was she. And we have lived irreproachably for many years. The punishment for that sin has come upon us now; and on which of us is the expiation to fall? . . .

"Can I give her up? If I do, my heart will break; but my heart must not decide. I must not think of myself; but try to find out whether it would not be a sin against God and the law. Ought I to let my wife leave me, and become the mistress of a Christian, or even become a Christian herself? Ought I to bring such shame upon the name of our God and upon his people?"

He drew himself up to his full height, and stretched out his hand toward heaven: "Though my heart and hers should break, Thy name shall not be dishonored, my Lord and my God."

His hand fell slowly, and he paused. "Alas!" he whispered, "has not Thy name even now been dishonored? Has she not spread her hands out to Thee above the lights in my house, with the image of the Christian in her heart? Could any sin be greater? Is it Thy will that this wickedness should go on for the rest of our lives? Is it Thy will, O God?"

He sat down, and bent his head upon the table. "I do not know what to do," he exclaimed aloud. "Help me, O God! Thou hast revealed Thy will through Thy priests and Thy prophets. I will study the law."

He went to the bookcase and took out a large folio. As he did so, a little book that had been lying behind it fell on the floor. He did not observe it, and carried the folio to the table, opened it, and began to read.

He read for a long time, consulting different parts of it. At last he closed the book sharply, stood up, and resting his clinched fist heavily upon it, said, mournfully :

"The law does not help me ; there is nothing in it at all applicable to a case such as this. The oldest law ordains that 'she should be stoned.' And the law of the Talmud is this : 'Let her die because of her sin, if the laws of the land in which ye live permit. If not, let the guilty woman be thrust out of her husband's house, and let her return to her father, who shall then punish and correct her as shall seem good in his eyes. She shall be without honor and without rights, excluded from all inheritance, and deprived of family ties.' . . .

"The law does not apply to us," he repeated. "She has been weak, not criminal. She has not deceived me—she is mine ; but, alas ! her heart does not belong to me. It never did, and I never thought of trying to make it mine. The law does not apply ; and who can show me a higher law ? "

Sighing deeply, he replaced the folio on the shelf, but when he tried to close the doors of the bookcase, he found that the little volume which had fallen unobserved prevented his doing so. He picked it up and looked at it. Memories of the past came back in a flood as he recognized the German book he had read so often as a youth. He had never quite understood its contents, and yet had studied it again and again, because of the sympathetic emotion it aroused in him. Schiller's poems, which he had laid aside for so many years, came into his hands again at this dark hour of his life. . . .

He sat down at the table, opened the book, and began to read. His youthful days returned vividly to his mind. One poem he had read beneath the old oak-tree in the park, and another he had surreptitiously studied in a corner of the cellar when he was overlooking his father's workmen. As he read on, he found to his surprise that he understood the whole meaning of the poems, and yet he had learned nothing new since these old days, except perhaps the secrets of the wine-trade. Each poem made a deep impression on him. It was so different from all that he had found in it before ! Whether better or worse he did not stop to inquire ; but the influence must have been good, for his heart felt relieved of the load that had oppressed it.

He rose and walked about the room in the stillness of the early Sabbath, repeating in a whisper some of the words he had just read. The only sound that was to be heard was the sputtering of one or other of the numerous wax-lights, or the fall of a heavy rain-drop against the window-pane.

. . . .

Morning came at last. The rain had ceased falling, and the last clouds were being driven by the wind across the leaden sky. In the east the sun was beginning to redden, and send its first bright rays upon the sodden plain : it had also penetrated to Nathan's parlor.

It found him still awake, but he was no longer restless, or speaking to himself. He stood quietly by the window, his face turned toward the east. The reflection of the sunrise lighted up his pale worn face, on which the calmness and peace of determined action were expressed. His eyes were fixed steadily on the east, and he seemed to be praying, though his lips did not move.

He had stood there a long time communing with God in the silence of the early morning.

The other inmates of the house began to stir. The servants held whispered consultations ; they guessed that something unusual had happened.

Chane left her room. Her face was pale, and her eyes were red with weeping. She approached Nathan with bent head.

"Chane," he said, gently, "I have made up my mind. I hope that what I mean to do will be for the best for you—and for him. As for me, our God is a merciful God—He will not forsake me."

He spoke the last words in so low a voice that she did not hear them. She blushed deeply, but did not speak. A moment later she hurried from the room,

6

and after a long absence, returned with his breakfast.

That done, they went to the synagogue together
as usual ; and no one seeing them had the least idea
of the agony of heart they were both enduring.

"Thank God! there is nothing wrong," said old
Jutta to the other maid-servant when she saw them
come home together, and sit down to their dinner as
usual.

Nathan soon rose, saying, "Be not afraid. I am
going to speak to him now. You shall know our decision in half an hour."

He went up-stairs to the rooms occupied by Herr
von Negrusz. The district judge was seated at his
writing-table. He seemed confused when he saw the
husband of the woman he loved. He expected a pain-
ful scene.

Nathan's manner was very quiet, and after a courteous greeting, he said : "Herr von Negrusz, your confusion shows that you know the reason of my visit.
You wrote this letter to my wife, but before I give
you the answer, tell me—why did you do it ? Is not
the commandment, 'Thou shalt not covet thy neighbor's wife,' as binding upon you as upon me ? "

" Yes," answered Herr von Negrusz, "I know that
I am guilty of a great sin—I love your wife. I make
no excuse for myself."

" I am glad you have answered so candidly," said

Nathan. "I have nothing further to say, except to give you the answer to your letter. My wife returns your love, therefore she can not be my wife any longer ; and I shall take the proper steps to obtain a divorce. What shall you do then, Herr von Negrusz ? "

"So help me God, I will marry her ! " he replied, earnestly.

Nathan looked at him keenly. " Good," he said. "I have no doubt that you intend to do so, for you are an honorable man ; but you are a Government official, a Christian, and of noble birth. She is only a Jewess. You are educated ; Chane is not. You may afterward be influenced by these considerations, and repudiate your present plan of action. I must guard against your doing so ; for Chane was my wife, and the moment she leaves me for your sake, her father and the whole Jewish community will cast her off. Should you break your promise, I shall take her back, for I—but enough of that. I tell you plainly, if you do not marry her, *I will kill you, so help me God!* You are the district judge, and I am nothing but a Jew. You have a hundred means at your disposal of getting rid of me, but I will keep my word."

Herr von Negrusz raised his hand, and was about to protest, but Nathan interrupted him hastily : " Do not swear," he said, " but keep your word, so that I may not have to keep mine. Chane and I will be

divorced in a few days, and if she is not your wife
before the end of two months, you are a dead man.
Farewell."

He went home and said to his wife : " We will go
to the Rabbi to-morrow, and tell him that we have
an insurmountable dislike to each other, and he will
at once give us a divorce on that account. The Christian has promised to marry you. Had that not been
his intention before, it is now. . . ."

"Nathan ! " she cried, throwing herself at his feet,
and covering his hand with tears and kisses—" Nathan,
how good you are ! "

"No," he answered, "I am not good. I am only
doing what I consider to be my duty. I am atoning
for a sin that was committed through no fault of
mine. We were married without our feelings being
consulted. That was a sin, and it is expiated now ;
for I love you, although perhaps I did not know it
until yesterday, and you do not love me—but another.
I can not doom you to misery ; rather than do that, I
suffer myself. This is the plain state of the case, and
I claim no merit for what I am doing. What distresses me most is that you will leave our faith, and
that I enable you to do so. I have prayed so earnestly to God for pardon, that I hope He will forgive
me. He sees my heart, and He knows that I have no
choice."

     *   *   *   *   *   *   *

There is little more to tell.

Nathan obtained a divorce in the course of a few days, and a few weeks after, Chane—now Christine—married Herr von Negrusz.

There had not been such a scandal in the neighborhood for years. Curses and malevolence followed Chane to her new home ; and even those who wished her well, shook their heads over the marriage.

The reader already knows that the curses were fruitless, and the fears of the benevolent unfounded. That Chane lived, a happy wife and mother, in the same house, on the threshold of which Esther Freudenthal had died because she had loved a Christian. This time love had triumphed over creed. It seemed to work miracles : for not only did it overleap barriers, but in spite of the objectionable features of the case, and the dissimilarity of the husband and wife, theirs was a happy marriage. For theirs was true love, and true love is a mighty power, a divine gift, without which it is a sin against God and man to enter into any marriage.

Christine von Negrusz has only one sorrow. It is not that Frau Emilie will hardly speak to her, or that the three elderly "Graces" look the other way when they chance to meet ; nor is it the sardonic smile with which Herr von Bolwinski accompanies the words—"I was the first to notice it, ho, ho !" whenever he has the opportunity. None of these things distress her; but a real shadow lies upon her otherwise happy life.

This is the wrath of her father, which will probably never cease until the lonely, disappointed old man finds peace in the grave.

Nathan took great pains to save her this one sorrow, but he was not successful. He does not yet give up hope of a reconciliation, and every time he revisits Barnow, he tries to soften the old man's heart.

But Nathan is seldom at Barnow, and when he returns there two or three times in the year, his visits are short. His business in the little town is managed for him by a cousin, and he travels to distant countries. He is no longer a small shopkeeper, but one of the richest wine-merchants in the country.

He has never married again. Once it was supposed that he was engaged to a girl in Czernowitz, but it was not the case. Only one person knew the reason of his solitude, and this was Frau Christine.

This she learned the only time she ever saw him to speak to after their separation. Nathan and Herr von Negrusz always met with friendly feelings, and when the former was at home, the two boys were continually with him; but he had avoided any meeting with Christine until now. It was at the time that people said that he was going to be married again. The boys were sitting with Nathan on the bench at the house-door, and as it was late, their mother came to fetch them. They ran to meet her, showed her the presents Nathan had brought for them, and dragged her up to the bench.

"I must thank you, Herr Silberstein," she said, in a trembling voice ; but she corrected herself quickly, and went on—"I must thank you, Nathan, for being so kind to the children."

"They are such dear little boys," he said, hastily. "I am very glad, Chane, to see you so happy."

"Yes," she answered, "I am very happy — and you ?"

"Thank you," he said, quietly ; "the business is prospering."

"The other day I heard some good news about you—from Czernowitz."

"There is nothing in it," he answered.

"Oh, why ? She is said to be a good and pretty girl."

He looked at her, and then on the ground. "I found that I could not love her," he said.

Many years have passed since then, and Nathan is one of the richest men in the country. People wonder why he works so hard when he has no one to leave his riches to. But Nathan smiles at such questions—he knows that he is working for some one.

TWO SAVIOURS OF THE PEOPLE.

(1870.)

TWO SAVIOURS OF THE PEOPLE.

ANY one who was ever in Barnow was sure to make the acquaintance of Frau Hanna, mother of the chief of the Jewish session; and no one could know her without honestly liking and admiring her, she was so good and kind, and so very quick in understanding and entering into the thoughts and feelings of others. But it would be difficult to convey an adequate idea of her loving-kindness and wisdom to those who never knew her. She was called *Babele* (grannie) by everybody who lived in the little town, and· not merely by her own grandchildren; and no wonder. She was never too busy or too tired to help those who needed her assistance either in word or deed; and even those who did not require money or advice used to delight in going to see her, and in hearing her stories of old times; for her renown as a story-teller was as great as her reputation for benevolence. Any one passing the old synagogue or *judenburg* about the third hour on a Sabbath afternoon in summer, might see with

his own eyes what a crowd of attentive listeners she
had, and might hear with his own ears how well
worth listening to her stories always were. She used
to sit on a rug spread out in the shade, with her
silent eager auditors, who sometimes numbered fifty
men and women, grouped closely around her for fear
of losing a single word that fell from her lips. Her
stories were all about old days in Barnow — about
things that had happened within her own memory, or
that she had heard from others. Any attempt to re-
produce her stories as she used to relate them would
be very difficult, and if I try to do so, it is only because the tale I have chosen is the one she related
far oftener than any other. I have heard her tell it
scores of times, and will now endeavor to translate it
from the Jewish-German in which she used to speak
as faithfully as I can:

"Who is great," began Frau Hanna, "and who is
small? Who is mighty, and who is weak? We poor
short-sighted mortals are seldom capable of deciding
this question rightly. The rich and strong are mighty
and great in our eyes, while the poor and feeble are
regarded as weak and small. But in very truth it is
not so. Greatness does not lie in riches or in brute
strength, but a strong will and a good heart. And, my
friends, God sometimes shows us this very clearly;
indeed, we Jews of Barnow can tell how our eyes were
opened to this truth. On two different occasions our

community was plunged in great danger and suffering
from the oppression of the Gentiles around us, and on
each of these occasions a saviour came forward from
among us, and delivering us from our distresses, turned
our mourning into joy. Who were these saviours of
the people? Were they the strongest or the richest
of the congregation? . . . Listen to me and I will
tell you how it all happened.

"When you cross the market-place, you see a great
big block of wood sticking out of the ground in front
of the Dominican monastery. It is weather-beaten and
decayed, and would have been taken away long ago,
were it not kept as a memorial of a time of terror
and despair.

"You know nothing of those old days, and you
may be thankful for it! If I tell you about that
time of misery, it is not that I wish to make your
hearts heavy with grief for what is past and gone, or
to fill them with bitter anger or hate. No; the sorrows of which I speak are over and done with, and
those who suffered from them are dead and buried.
It is written among the sayings of one of our wise
and holy men: 'Forgive those who have trespassed
against you, and return good for evil.' What I am
going to tell you is the history of a great and noble
deed that was done by one who lived and suffered
during that time of dire distress—a deed that should
make your hearts beat high when you hear of it, for

it is as heroic, good, and great as was ever done on the face of the earth.

"Its author was a simple Jewish woman, whose heart had been steeled to heroism by the force of circumstances. Her name was Lea, and she was the wife of a rich and pious man called Samuel. The family was afterward given the surname of Beermann when the Austrians came into the country, and made it the law that our people should have German names as well as their old ones; for at the time when these events took place we had no such names. It was more than a hundred years ago, and we were still living under the rule of the Polish nobles.

"The single-headed white eagle was indeed a cruel bird of prey! Long ago, when it was full-plumaged, when its eyes were clear and piercing, and its talons firm and relentless in their grip, it was a proud and noble bird that held its own against both West and North, and protected all who took refuge under its wing most generously. For three hundred years we lived a free and happy life under the shadow of its wings; but when the eagle grew old and weak, and the other birds of prey round about had deprived it of many of its feathers, it became cowardly, sly, and cruel; and because it did not dare to attack its enemies, it turned its wrath upon the defenseless Jews. The power of the kings of Poland became a subject for children to jest about, and then the letters of freedom we had been given of old were no longer of any avail. The nobles became our masters. They oppressed us, extorted money from us, and disposed of our lives and property as it seemed good in their eyes. Oh, that was a time of unspeakable tribulation!

"Barnow belonged even then to the noble family of Bortynski, to whom the good Emperor Joseph afterward gave the title of Graf. Young Joseph Bortynski had entered into possession of his estate that very year. He was a quiet, pious, humble-minded man, and had been educated in a cloister. His ways were different from those of the other young men of his position in the neighborhood, for he hated wine, cards, and women, looked after the management of his property, and prayed four hours a day. He was just and kind in his dealings with his serfs; but we experienced very little of his kindness and justice, for he was hard and cruel to us. He once gave Samuel, the leader of the synagogue, his reason for treating us so badly: 'You crucified my God,' he said. Whenever he was inclined to act toward us with less harshness, he was prevented doing so by his private chaplain, a man who had formerly been his tutor, and who had great influence over him. His name has not come down to us, but he was always talked of as the 'black priest.'

"We Jews used to be very careful of our conduct in those days, and even those of our number who were evil-disposed refrained from deeds of wickedness.

'You crucified my God,' the Graf had said to Samuel, and had then added in a threatening tone : 'I give you fair warning, that if I find any of your people guilty of a crime, I shall burn your town as your God once did to Sodom and Gomorrah.' Our fears may be better imagined than described.

"So the spring of 1773 began. The Easter festival was about to commence, when it was rumored that the Empress-Queen at Vienna intended to deprive the Poles of their remaining power, and to govern the land henceforward by means of her own officials. But so far as we could see, there was no sign of this intention being carried out.

"Samuel, the leader of the synagogue, and his wife Lea, lived in the old house in the market-place that is still known as the 'yellow house.' They were both very much respected by the community : the husband, because of his riches, wisdom, and piety ; and the beautiful young wife, because of her gentleness and beneficence. They were in great trouble that Easter, for their only child, a little boy of a year and a half old, had died suddenly a few days before.

"Late one Sunday evening they were sitting together in silent grief. The Easter festival was to begin on the following evening, and Lea was very tired, for she had been busy all day long cleaning and dusting the whole house from top to bottom. Suddenly they were startled by a loud knocking at the house-

door. Samuel opened the window and looked out.
An old peasant-woman was standing at the door with
a bundle on her back. On seeing the master of the
house, she moaned out a piteous entreaty for admit-
tance. She was too weak, she said, to walk home to
her village that evening, and so she begged Samuel to
give her shelter for the night.

"'This isn't an inn,' answered Samuel, shortly, at
the same time shutting the window.

"'Poor thing,' said Lea, 'ought we to send her
away?'

"'We're living in dangerous times,' replied Samuel; 'I don't like to admit a stranger into my house.'

"'But this poor creature is ill and weak,' said Lea.

"And as the old woman outside continued to make
an appeal to his pity, Samuel gave way and let her in.
The maid-servants were all in bed and asleep, so Lea
took her guest to a garret-room, and, after providing her
with food and wine, wished her good-night, and left her.

"Next morning the stranger took leave of her hostess very early, and with many expressions of gratitude.
Lea was so busy all day making the final preparations
for the feast, that she had not time to visit the room
that had been occupied by the old woman until late in
the afternoon, when she was making a last round of the
house to see that no leavened bread was anywhere to
be found. The room was perfectly neat and tidy, but
she was astonished to find it pervaded by a most disa-

greeable smell. She opened the window, but that'had
no effect. She hunted about for the cause of the horrible odor. At length, on looking under the bed, she
saw what made her blood run cold and her hair stand
on end with terror. For under the bed there lay the
naked corpse of a half-starved little child, with great
wounds in its neck and chest. Lea at once understood
what had happened, and struggled hard against the
faintness that threatened to overpower her. The old
woman had brought the corpse to the house, and had
concealed it there, in order· that the hideous old story
might be revived that the Jews were in the habit of
killing Christian children before the feast of the Pass-
over ; and terrible would be the vengeance taken by
the Christians of the neighborhood. Lea recognized
the full horrors of her position, and remembered the
Graf's warning to her husband. She was nearly over-
whelmed with the weight of her misery. For was it
not she, and she alone, who, by inducing her husband
to admit the woman into the house, had brought all the
sorrow, persecution, and death that would surely come
upon her home and upon the whole Jewish community ?
While she sat there shivering with fever and anguish,
she heard wild cries, shrieks, and the sound of weeping
in the street, and also the clank of swords. 'They are
coming,' she muttered, and at the same moment a
thought flashed into her mind, far more strange and
horrible than a woman's brain had ever before con-

ceived, and yet so noble and self-sacrificing that a woman alone could have entertained it. 'It was my fault,' she said to herself, 'and I alone must bear the consequences.' She rose to her feet, pressed her lips firmly together, and after a struggle regained her composure. Then taking up the child's corpse, she wrapped it in a linen cloth and laid it on her knee.

"She listened ; . . . the minutes seemed to drag. Then she heard the young Graf's voice outside speaking passionately to her husband and another member of the session in these words : ' The woman heard the death-rattle distinctly. I will not leave one stone upon another if I find the body.' She heard the men going through all the rooms in the house. As their steps approached the one in which she was seated, she rose and went to the window, below which the roof fell away steeply, and overhung the paved court-yard of the house.

"The door was thrown open violently ; the Graf entered, accompanied by the two members of session, and followed by his men-at-arms. Lea sprang forward to meet them with a wild laugh, showed them the child's body, and then flung it out of the window on to the court beneath. . . .

" 'I am a murderess,' she cried out to the Graf ; 'yes, I am, I am. Take me, bind me, kill me ! I murdered my own child last night ; I don't deny it. You've come to fetch me ; here I am !'

"The men stared at her in speechless amazement.

"Then came furious cries, shouts, and questions. Samuel, strong man as he was, fainted away. The other Jews, at once perceiving the true state of the case, and seeing no other way of saving the whole community from certain death, supported her in her statement. Lea remained firm. The Graf looked at her piercingly, and she returned his gaze without flinching : 'Listen, woman,' he said ; 'if you have really committed the crime of which you have confessed yourself guilty, you shall die a death of torture far more terrible than any one has ever yet suffered ; but if the other Jews killed the child in order to drink its blood at the feast, you and your husband shall go unpunished, and the others shall alone expiate their crime. I swear this by all that is holy ! Now— choose !'

"Lea did not hesitate for a moment. 'It was my child,' she said.

"The Graf had Lea taken to prison and confined in a solitary cell. He quite saw all the improbability of her story, but he did not believe in any greatness of soul in one of our people. 'If it were not true, he thought, 'why should the woman have given herself up ?'

"The trial threw no light upon the subject.

"All the Jewish witnesses bore testimony against Lea. One told how she had hated her child ; another how she had threatened to kill it. Fear of death forced these lies from their lips. The only Christian witness was the black priest's housekeeper—the same woman who had gone to Samuel's house on that fatal evening in the disguise of a peasant to bring destruction on the Jewish community. She told how she had heard the death-rattle of the child during the night. She could not say more without betraying herself, and so her story tallied with Lea's confession. The 'black priest' took no apparent interest in the trial. He probably thought that one victim would suffice for the time, or it may be that he feared the discovery of his crime.

"The Graf's judges pronounced Lea guilty, and condemned her to be broken on the wheel in the market-place, and there beheaded. The wooden block in front of the Dominican monastery was placed there for this purpose.

"But Lea did not die on the scaffold; she died peacefully in her own house forty years later, surrounded by her children and grandchildren; for Austrian military law was proclaimed in the district before Graf Bortynski's people had had time to execute the sentence pronounced upon Lea, and an Austrian Government official, whose duty it was to try criminal cases, examined the evidence against her. Samuel went to him and told him the whole story, and he, after due inquiry, set Lea free.

"The wooden block is still standing. It reminds us of the old dark days of our oppression. But it also reminds us of the noble and heroic action by which a weak woman saved the community. . . .

"And eighty years after that, my friends—eighty years after that—when we were once more in danger of losing our lives, who was it that saved us? Not a woman this time; but a timid little man whom no one could have imagined capable of a courageous action, and whose name I have only to mention to send you into a fit of laughter. It was little Mendele. . . . Ah, see now how you are chuckling! Well, well, I can't blame you, for he is a very queer little man. He knows many a merry tale, and tells them very amusingly. And then it is certainly a very strange thing to see a gray-haired man no taller than a child, and with the ways and heart of a child. He used to dance and sing all day long. I don't think that any one ever saw him quiet. Even now he does not walk down a street, but trots instead; he does not talk, but sings, and his hands seem to have been given him for no other use but to beat time. But—what of that? It is better to keep a cheerful heart than to wear a look of hypocritical solemnity. Mendele Abenstern is a great singer, and we may well be proud of having him for our *chazzán* (deacon). It is true that he sometimes rattles off a touching prayer as if it were a waltz, and that when reading the Thorah he fidgets about from one leg to the other as if he were a dancer at a theatre. But these little peculiarities of his never interfere with our devotions, for we have been accustomed to Mendele and his ways for the last forty years, and if any one happens to get irritated with him now and then, he takes care not to vent it on the manikin. He can not help remembering, you see, that little Mendele can be grave enough at times, and that the poor *chazzân* once did the town greater service by his gift of song than all the wise and rich could accomplish by their wisdom or their wealth.

"I will tell you how that came to pass.

"You know that a Jew is looked upon nowadays as a man like every one else; and that if any noble or peasant dares to strike or oppress a Jew, the latter can at once bring his assailant before the Austrian district judge at the court-hall, and Herr von Negrusz punishes the offender for his injustice. But before the great year when the Emperor proclaimed that all men had equal rights, it was not so. In those old days, the lord of the manor exercised justice within the bounds of his territory by means of his agent; but what was called justice by these men was generally great injustice. Ah, my friends, those were hard times! The land belonged to the lord of the manor, and so did all the people who lived on it; and the very air and water were his also. It was not only in the villages that this was the case, but in the towns too, especially when they belonged to a noble, and when their inhabitants were Jews. The noble was lord of all, and ruled over his subjects through his agent or *mandatar*.

"At least it was so with us in Barnow. Our master, Graf Bortynski, lived in Paris all the year round, and gave himself no trouble about his estates or their management. His agent was supreme in Barnow, and was to all intents and purposes our master. So we always used to pray that the *mandatar* might be a good man, who would allow us to live in peace and quietness. And at first God answered our prayers, for stout old Herr Stephan Grudza was as easy-tempered a man as we Jews could have desired. It's true that he used to drink from morning till night, but he was always good-natured in his cups, and would not for the world have made any one miserable when he was merry. But one day, after making a particularly good dinner, he was seized with apoplexy and died. The whole district mourned for him, and so did we Jews of Barnow. For, in the first place, Herr Grudza had been kind to every one ; and in the second—who knew what his successor would be like !

"Our fears were well grounded.

"The new *mandatar*, Friedrich Wollmann, was a German. Now the Germans had hitherto treated us less harshly than the Poles. The new agent, however,

was an exception to this rule.   He was a tall, thin
man, with black hair and bright black eyes.   His expression was stern and sad—always, always—no one
ever saw him smile.   He was a good manager, and
soon got the estate into order ; he also insisted on
the laws being obeyed ; taught evil-doers that he was
not a man to be trifled with ; and I am quite sure
that no one with whom he had any dealings defrauded
him of a halfpenny.   But he hated us Jews with a
deadly hatred, and did us all as much harm as he
could.   He increased our taxes threefold—sent our
sons away to be soldiers—disturbed our feasts—and
whenever we had a lawsuit with a Christian, the Christian's word was always taken, while ours was disbe-
lieved.   He was very hard upon the peasants too—in
fact, they said that no other agent at Barnow had
ever been known to exact the *robot* due from the vil-
lein to his lord with so much severity, and yet in that
matter he acted within the letter of the law ; and so
there was a sort of justice in his mode of procedure.
But as soon as he had anything to do with a Jew, he
forgot both reason and justice.

"Why did he persecute us so vehemently ?   No
one knew for certain, but we all guessed.   It was said
that he used to be called Troim Wollmann, and that
he was a Christianized Jew from Posen ; that he had
forsworn his religion from love for a Christian girl,
and that the Jews of his native place had persecuted

7

and calumniated him so terribly in consequence of his
apostasy, that the girl's parents had broken off their
daughter's engagement to him. I do not know who
told us this, but no one could deny the probability
of the story who ever had looked him in the face, or
had watched the mode of treating us.

"So our days were sad and full of foreboding for
the future. Wollmann oppressed and squeezed us
whether we owed him money or not, and none that
displeased him had a chance of escape. Thus matters
stood in the autumn before the great year.

"It isn't the pleasantest thing in the world for a
Jew to be an Austrian soldier, but if one of our race
is sent into the Russian service his fate is worse than
death. He is thenceforward lost to God, to his parents, and to himself. Is it, then, a matter for surprise
that the Russian Jews should gladly spend their last
penny to buy their children's freedom from military
service, or that any youth, whose people are too poor
to ransom him, should fly over the border to escape
his fate? Many such cases are known : some of the
fugitives are caught before they have crossed the
frontiers of Russia, and it would have been better
for them if they had never been born ; but some
make good their escape into Moldavia, or into our
part of Austrian Poland. Well, it happened that
about that time a Jewish conscript—born at Berdie-
zow—escaped over the frontier near Hussintyn, and

was sent on to Barnow from thence. The community did what they could for him, and a rich,
kind-hearted man, Chaim Grünstein, father-in-law of
Moses Freudenthal, took him into his service as
groom.

"The Russian Government of course wanted to get
the fugitive back into their hands, and our officials
received orders to look for him. •

"Our *mandatar* got the same order as the others.
He at once sent for the elders of our congregation
and questioned them on the subject. They were inwardly much afraid, but outwardly they made no sign,
and denied all knowledge of the stranger. It was on
the eve of the Day of Atonement that this took place
—and how could they have entered the presence of
God that evening if they had betrayed their brother
in the faith? So they remained firm in spite of the
agent's threats and rage. When he perceived that
they either knew nothing or would confess nothing,
he let them go with these dark words of warning:
'It will be the worse for you if I find the youth in
Barnow. You do not know me yet, but—I swear that
you shall know me then!'

"The elders went home, and I need hardly tell
you that the hearts of the whole community sank
on hearing Wollmann's threat. The young man
they were protecting was a hard-working honest
fellow, but even if he had been different, it wouldn't

have mattered—he was a Jew, and none of them
would have forsaken him in.his adversity. If he remained in Barnow, the danger to him and to all of
them was great, for the *mandatar* would find him
out sooner or later—nothing could be kept from him
for long. But if they sent him away without a
passport or naturalization papers, he would of course
be arrested very soon. After a long consultation,
Chaim Grünstein had a happy inspiration. One of
his relations was a tenant - farmer in Marmaros, in
Hungary. The young man should be sent to him
on the night following the Day of Atonement, and
should be desired to make the whole journey by
night for fear of discovery. In this manner he could
best escape from his enemies.

"They all agreed that the idea was a good one, and
then partook with lightened hearts of the feast which
was to strengthen them for their fast on the Day of
Atonement. Dusk began to fall. The synagogue was
lighted up with numerous wax-candles, and the whole
community hastened there with a broken and a con-
trite heart to confess their sins before God; for at
that solemn fast we meet to pray to the Judge of all
men to be gracious to us, and of His mercy to forgive us our trespasses. The women were all dressed
in white, and the men in white grave-clothes. Chaim
Grünstein and his household were there to humble
themselves before the Lord, and among them was

the poor fugitive, who was trembling in every limb with fear lest he should fall into the hands of his enemies.

"All were assembled, and divine service was about to begin. Little Mendele had placed the flat of his hand upon his throat in order to bring out the first notes of the 'Kol-Nidra' with fitting tremulousness, when he was interrupted by a disturbance at the door. The entrance of the synagogue was beset by the Graf's men-at-arms, and Herr Wollmann was seen walking up the aisle between the rows of seats. The intruder advanced until he stood beside the ark of the covenant and quite close to little Mendele, who drew back in terror, but the elders of the congregation came forward with quiet humility.

"'I know that the young man is here,' said Wollmann; 'will you give him up now?'

"The men were silent.

"'Very well,' continued the *mandatar*, 'I see that kindness has no effect upon you. I will arrest him after service when you leave the synagogue. And I warn you that both he and you shall have cause to remember this evening. But now, don't let me disturb you; go on with your prayers. I have time to wait.'

"A silence as of death reigned in the synagogue. It was at length broken by a shrill cry from the women's gallery. The whole congregation was at first stupefied with fear. But after a time every one began to regain his self-command, and to raise his eyes to God for help. Without a word each went back to his seat.

"Little Mendele trembled in every limb; but all at once he drew himself up and began to sing the 'Kol-Nidra,' that ancient simple melody, which no one who has ever heard can forget. His voice at first sounded weak and quavering, but it gradually gained strength and volume, filled the edifice, thrilled the hearts of all the worshipers, and rose up to the throne of God. Little Mendele never again sang as he did that evening. He seemed as though he were inspired. When he was singing in that marvelous way, he ceased to be the absurd little man he had always hitherto been, and became a priest pleading with God for his people. He reminded us of the former glories of our race, and then of the many, many centuries of ignominy and persecution that had followed. In the sound of his voice we could hear the story of the way in which we had been chased from place to place—never suffered to rest long anywhere; of how we were the poorest of the poor, the most wretched among the miserable of the earth; and how the days of our persecution were not yet ended, but ever new oppressors rose against us and ground us down with an iron hand. The tale of our woes might be heard in his voice—of our unspeakable woes and our innumerable tears. But there was something else to be heard in it too. It told us in triumphant tones of our pride in our nation, and of our confidence and *trust in God.* Ah me! I can never describe the way little Mendele sang that evening; he made us weep for our desolation, and yet restored our courage and our trust. . . .

"The women were sobbing aloud when he ceased; even the men were weeping; but little Mendele hid his face in his hands and fainted.

"At the beginning of the service Wollmann had kept his eyes fixed on the ark of the convenant, but as it went on he had to turn away. He was very pale, and his knees shook so that, strong man as he was, he could hardly stand. His eyes shone as though through tears. With trembling steps and bowed head he slowly passed Mendele, and walked down the aisle to the entrance-door. Then he gave the soldiers a sign to follow him.

"Every one guessed what had happened, but no one spoke of it.

"He sent for Chaim Grünstein on the day after the fast, and, giving him a blank passport, said, 'It will perhaps be useful to you.'

"From that time forward he treated us with greater toleration; but his power did not last long. The peasants, whom he had formerly oppressed, rose against him in the spring of the Great Year, and put him to death. . . .

"Now, my friends, this is the story of the Two Saviours of the Jews of Barnow. Let it teach you to think twice before saying who is great and who is small, who is weak and who is mighty!"

"THE CHILD OF ATONEMENT."

(1872.)

"THE CHILD OF ATONEMENT."

THE heroine of this story is a child. Her name was Lea, and at the time of which the story treats, she was four years old. She had glossy black hair and large dark eyes. Her eyes, however, were not bright, for it seemed as if a shadow lay on her pale delicate face. She was the child of poor people, and had only one frock, which was patched all over —the same for Saturdays as for the other days of the week. It was hardly possible to distinguish the original color of the yellow gabardine.

But that was not the cause of the sadness of her expression, for what did Lea know of poverty? Every day her appetite was satisfied, or at any rate half satisfied; and every day she played in the sunshine as long as she liked.

She had the most beautiful playground that could be desired—large, green, quiet, and full of countless flowers, and of elders bowing their blossom-laden heads over many resting-places. Lea's playground was the Jewish cemetery at Barnow. It was strange to see the serious child wandering among the graves, or sitting on a stone watching the merry cockchafers running about in the grass; but this was not the cause of the shade of sadness on her face.

What did Lea know of death? She knew that her father was dead, and that death meant sleep, and never, never to be hungry more. How, then, could the daily sight of the graves have saddened her? . . .

No, it had not; and the Jews of Barnow were also wrong when they said, "The child is a child of atonement; how can its face be otherwise than sad?"

No; every trace of suffering in her pale face was an inheritance.

Poor Miriam Goldstein had borne the child beneath a heart that was heavy with grief and sorrow. Bitter tears had fallen upon the face of the little creature that lay upon her bosom. Such tears dry, but they leave their traces. Lea bore upon her countenance the marks of the tears shed by her mother.

Later, as the child grew older, her mother ceased to weep. The poor widow had no time for tears. She had to work all day long, and when she came home at night, she sank exhausted on her bed.

Even when she wakened, and mused upon her hard sad lot, she did not weep, for she could always comfort herself with the reflection, "Thank God! the child and I are not obliged to beg or starve. Thank God! the child is well."

"The child is well."

Miriam Goldstein, widow of the gravedigger at Barnow, who received from the community as her widow's portion the grant of a little room in the cottage near the gate of the cemetery, and who worked in other people's houses all day long, did not weep during any sleepless hours that might come to her at night, because—her child was well. I ask all mothers —had Miriam Goldstein any cause for tears?

The days came and went. Little Lea was now four years old. She played on the grave-mounds during the long, bright summer days, crept about under the branches of the elder bushes quietly and happily, and beneath the clothes which her mother had hung up in long lines above the graves to dry.

Soon autumn came with its long damp evenings. It became dark early, and when Miriam was detained till a late hour, Lea used to wait for her patiently in their little room. She knew that ere long she would hear her mother's step outside, and her voice calling her as she opened the door. She could then run into her arms, and a fire would soon be burning to cook a warm supper.

But once, on a raw, cold September night, it was not so. The washerwoman came home and called her child, but no answer came.

Trembling, she struck a light. The room was empty.

"Lea!" she cried again, loudly and sharply.

Still no answer. She let her hands fall helplessly at her sides. Recovering herself quickly, she rushed into the room of her neighbor, the gravedigger who had formerly been under her husband, and who had succeeded to his place.

"My child!" she cried; "where is my child?"

The man and his wife stared at her as if she were mad.

"How should we know?" they at length answered, with hesitation.

"She is gone! Oh, help me, help me!" the mother cried in desperation, as she turned and hurried out into the dark burial-ground.

The gravedigger's wife searched the highroad which leads toward the town, while the man followed Miriam.

He distinguished her dark figure amongst the mounds and headstones, but he was unable to overtake her. She was running wildly over every obstacle, now stepping on a gravestone, and again stumbling over the root of a tree, calling her child loudly as she ran. The man knew the place well, and its terrors had become commonplace in his eyes; but still his hair stood on end with fear, as he ran in the dark over the graves, and the mother's despairing cry fell on his ears.

They both neared the spot where the burial-ground is bounded by the deep, sluggish river Lered. "The fence is broken," muttered the man, and he tried not to follow up the thought that had occurred to him.

But fate had been merciful.

As they hastened along by the side of the fence, and Miriam, with an almost failing voice, called her child, suddenly, from behind a gravestone, a thin trembling voice answered—"Mother!"

The little girl had run about the whole day When the dusk had surprised her in this distant place, she had sat down and fallen asleep.

The child only half comprehended why her mother seized her hastily in her arms, and pressed her to her breast, covering her little face with a thousand kisses and tears.

Slowly Miriam carried her home, the gravedigger following and rejoicing, while he shook his head, and murmured: "It wouldn't have surprised me had we found the child dead. Not at all! The Great Death is coming near us again. They say that it has already reached the Turks! . . ."

Miriam did not hear these strange words. She carried the child into her little room, and put her in bed even more tenderly than usual, smoothing her hair off her brow, and kissing her mouth again and again.

Then she visited her neighbors, and thanked them in woman's fashion, in many words. After that, she returned to her own room, and thanked God with a long silent look upward.

She could not sleep, so she crouched beside the bed, and watched her sleeping child. But, heavens! what was the matter? The poor woman's blood turned cold, for Lea's usually pale face was flushed with fever, and she was breathing quickly and ster-torously. Her hands and feet were cold, and her head was burning hot.

"Lea, are you ill?" cried Miriam. "Speak, my life!"

Hearing her voice, the child opened her eyes, but they were no longer lusterless. A strange unnatural light glowed in them. "I am cold," she lisped, draw-ing the bed-clothes about her.

"She will die! . . ." was Miriam's muttered thought, and she felt paralyzed for the moment. Re-covering herself, however, she took her thin shawl from her shoulders, and her best gown from her box, and spread them over the child. Lea's teeth were chattering. She shivered with cold, though she seemed but half conscious.

Miriam once more hurried to her neighbors' room, and knocked at their closed door. She wished to beg them to come and tell her what was the matter with her child ; for a Jewish gravedigger is required to visit the sick as well as to bury the dead. When the doctor is not called in, the gravedigger is sent for. But the man had gone to the town to keep the night-watch over the body of rich Moses Freudenthal. His wife came, however, and staid with the poor widow, in hopes of comforting her.

"It is only a fever," she said, consolingly. "The child has caught cold, and it is only a common fever. See, burning heat follows a shivering fit."

In fact, Lea's fever soon ran so high, that all her bed-clothes had to be taken off. The women made a strong herb tea, but the child would not drink it.

The terrible night passed very slowly.

In the morning, when the gravedigger came home from his sad vigil, he went to see the sick child. On seeing her, he shook his head. The mother wrung her hands in despair when she saw his gesture, and gave utterance to a low moan. He pitied her, and said slowly : "It isn't a dangerous kind of fever. Lea will soon be well."

"Tell me the truth," cried Miriam; "but I shall send for the doctor whether the illness is dangerous or not."

The gravedigger shrugged his shoulders. "The doctor has been at the muster at Zalesczyki for the last eight days. But even if he were here . . . No doctor can help the child!"

"Must she die?" asked Miriam.

"No *doctor*, I say," answered the gravedigger slowly, "but a holy rabbi might save her. Old Moses Freudenthal's funeral is to take place to-day, and our rabbi is going to attend. Ask him to see the child, and bless it. He is a holy man—perhaps he is strong enough to save it, and perhaps he will give you advice."

So saying, he went away to prepare the grave. His wife followed him.

"I may as well dig two graves," said he, as he struck his spade into the ground.

"You mean for the child?" asked his wife. "Poor Miriam—God spare her! . . ."

"Yes," he answered, "it makes my heart ache. But no man can save her. They say that the Great Death is coming again. God will spare us. He will only take the 'child of atonement' that we have delivered up to Him."

"In God's name," cried the woman, "why should an innocent life be taken."

The man shrugged his shoulders, and asked: "Would you pretend to be more holy than our holy rabbi? Are you more just than the great Reb Grolce, the wonder-working rabbi of Sadagóra, who has ordained it so"?

The woman was silent.

.   .   .   .

What had the wonder-working rabbi ordained? And why did they call the child a "child of atonement"?

. . . Mysteriously, irresistibly, the destroying-angel of the Lord brought un unknown plague into every land in the terrible year 1831. It was called the cholera. It came from the far East, and spread onward to the far West, devastating the towns, and filling the cemeteries. It fell heavily on the dirty, poverty-stricken villages in the Podolian plain. Countless numbers of the inhabitants died like flies, and enough were not left to bury the dead. No remedies saved life; no precautions protected it. Stolid resignation, or else angry desperation, possessed the people. And God permitted all this misery, and from God no help came! They called upon Him and He did not hear! . . .

Why? Why?

Was it not *their* God whom they implored, the God of their fathers, the almighty, the just, and the only God? Had He no longer ears to hear, or arms to help? Why did He suddenly turn against His own people? Why did He not protect the good and the just among them?

The minds of the unhappy people began to waver. They had but one beacon to direct their lives—their faith; and their faith betrayed them. They could not comprehend it.

Then another thought occurred to them—a fearful and crushing thought, and yet it brought comfort. Was not their God a God of vengeance? Was He not a jealous God, who exacted, for every offense, a fearful and inexorable atonement? And now, when He caused the evil and the good to suffer alike, was it not probably because the wicked sinned, and the good allowed their sins to pass unpunished?

"We will purify ourselves," the suffering people cried aloud in their agony. "We will seek the offender in our midst, and by his punishment we will atone, and save ourselves from the wrath of God. . . ."

And they purified themselves. . . .

A tribunal was formed by the people—an awful court, which tried in secret, judged in secret, and punished in secret. It was stern and inexorable in the execution of its decrees, and no one could escape from it. It "vindicated God's holy name," and caused the hour of retribution to strike for many criminals who had evaded the laws. But with how much innocent blood had these fanatics stained their hands! Deeds were done in those dark days of madness and terror that chill the blood, and make the historian, who attempts to describe them, falter.

The pestilence became more and more terrible. The few doctors that remained folded their hands. They could not alleviate the suffering of the people, far less could they save their lives.

Men ceased to persecute each other for real or imaginary sins. The growing burden of misfortune took away their spirit, and made them faint-hearted. They even prayed no longer ; a mediator had to pray for them.

The intercessor they chose was the rabbi of Sadagóra, a little town in Bukowina. This man was called the "wonder-worker," on account of all that he had done, or was supposed to have done, for the people. To him the Podolian Jews turned in their dire necessity, imploring him to save them, by beseeching God in his own name, a powerful name ; for it was believed that from his race the Redeemer was to spring : and it was said that he had upon the palms of his hands the stamp of the royal line of David. This mark was the outline of a lion imprinted upon the skin, and it was a sign that his mission was from God. Money and precious gifts were collected, and were given to the rabbi to insure his intercession with God ; even the poor gave all that they possessed.

The disinterested rabbi promised to help the people. "You have all sinned against God," he said, "and you must all do penance."

He made a calendar of the days of expiation, and the days of fasting and mortification were punctually kept. Fear of death insured the fulfillment of all his injunctions. It may sound incredible, but it is literally true, that during this time the whole Eastern Jewish population only ate and drank every second day.

The result of this may be easily imagined. Their weakened frames were all the more liable to be smitten by the disease.

The renown of the rabbi was at stake, and with it the profits of his calling. He adopted another expedient.

"God is pleased," he said, "by an increase of His faithful people. Let each community choose a couple from its number, and marry them in the burial-ground—as a sacrifice to the angry God."

This new remedy had different consequences. In many places, the assemblage of crowds of people in the graveyards, in order to be present at the marriage ceremonies, helped to spread the plague. In other places, however, the insane remedy was harmless, as the "Great Death" was already passing away, and was soon to become extinct.

This means of propitiation was not soon forgotten ; and in the year 1848, when, along with freedom, poverty came, bringing the "Great Death" in its train across the Eastern steppes, the panic-stricken people resorted to it again. These appalling marriages were solemnized everywhere.

One took place in Barnow. The unfortunate couple who were chosen—without any wish of their own, but by the will of the tyrants—to be endowed with a marriage-portion of misery, and to be made man and wife among the freshly dug graves, were Nathan Goldstein, the gravedigger, and Miriam Roth, a friendless orphan, and maid-servant in the house of the warden of the community. They saw each other for the first time when they plighted their troth under the open sky.

The couple, who were thus suddenly and horribly set apart to atone for the sins of the congregation, were resigned, and even happy. None knew better than these poor dependants how to appreciate the blessings of a home.

Miriam and Nathan were happy in their married life, and two children were born to them. Their first great grief was the loss of both of their children, who fell ill, and died within a few days of each other in the year 1859. God, however, repaired the loss, for in the spring of the following year, Miriam knew she was again to be a mother.

That summer, the destroying-angel once more came from the East, and brought a fearful scourge upon the neglected Jewish villages of the great Podolian plain.

Barnow was spared. One victim alone was taken —Nathan the gravedigger. The widow's grief knew no bounds, and she was left in an utterly helpless condition. The community, on the other hand, re-

joiced at their happy escape from the plague, which
died out altogether. They sent the good news, with
grateful thanks and presents, to Sadagóra, where the
son of the late wonder-working rabbi had succeeded
to his father's office. The rabbi accepted the gifts,
but declined the thanks ; and when the deputation
informed him of the one death that had taken place,
he said : "God was well pleased with you when He
withdrew the plague eleven years ago, after you had
made a sacrifice to Him ; but the people you chose
to dedicate to Him did not please Him, so their children died. Now the man has died as a sin-offering
for you all. If the woman has another child, it also
will only live to be a sin-offering.

So spoke the rabbi, for the gravedigger's widow
could give him no present. The men returned home
and reported what he had said.

Miriam heard of it, and wept bitterly. But she
had little time for weeping. She had to work hard
to keep herself and her child from starvation.

So the years passed, until the sad autumn of
1863 came. The Poles had risen against the great
Eastern nation, and a whispered rumor went through
the land, that pestilence, the terrible sister of war,
was again aroused.

Therefore the gravedigger did not believe that
little Lea, "the child of atonement," would live.

The funeral of old Moses Freudenthal was over. He was a very old man, and few mourners followed him to the grave. After the service was over, these went away immediately, and the old rabbi, also, did not linger. The widow had humbly waited for this moment to step forward and ask the rabbi to come and see her child. She added no word of entreaty, but something in the tone of her voice, and in the expression of her eyes, involuntarily touched the heart of the old man. This woman embarrassed him —for was she not displeasing to God? Was not the destiny of the child well known—this "child of atonement"? . . .

But he went to the little house, and entered the room where the sick child lay. He bent over the bed, and looked at her in silence for a length of time. His expression was stern and harsh when he raised his head.

With intense anxiety the mother waited for him to speak, but the old man turned to go without uttering a word.

"Will you not bless the child?" asked the widow.

"Woman," answered the rabbi, gloomily, "no blessing can save her; and besides, I can not do it: it would be interfering with the Almighty."

Miriam threw herself upon the bed, with a loud cry, clasping the unconscious child to her heart, as

8

though she would save her from every one, even from God. "Why," she cried, "why, rabbi?"

The old man looked at her darkly, then his eyes, as if confused, sought the ground. "You know," he said with hesitation, "why you and your husband were married. You know why he died, and what was the object of his death. You know the word that the great rabbi of Sadagóra has spoken concerning you and your child. And . . . now . . . the 'Great Death' is coming again . . ."

The woman understood him. "Ah," she whispered, in a low voice of indescribable scorn. With flaming eyes and glowing face she rose from the bed, so that she stood opposite the rabbi, and hissed out, "You lie, rabbi, you lie! My child shall not die! . . . God is wise, gracious, and just; but you, neither you, nor any of the others, are like God! You want to be just, and yet you demand that an innocent child should expiate your sins by its death! You want to be gracious, and yet you desire the death of another! You want to be wise, and yet you believe that God will allow this—our good, strong, just God!"

She clasped her hands over her forehead, tottered, and sank fainting on the floor.

"May God judge between you and me!" murmured the old man as he left the room.

A day and night passed, and it seemed as if God must quickly decide between the poor woman and the rabbi. It appeared as if He would be on the side of the rabbi, and of hard, stubborn mankind. When the gray light of the second morning dawned, and the flame of the night-light wavered in the draught of the cold autumn wind, which made its way through the badly fitting window-frame, the young life flickered under the icy breath of death, like a dying torch.

The mother wept no more.

She wept no more. The fountain of her tears was dried up, for the deepest grief is tearless. With dry, straining eyes she knelt by the bedside. Only at intervals, when the fever was at its height, she rose softly.

Hours passed, and all throughout the day the room was filled with visitors. A number of women came and went, and also a few men. Some of these may have come out of compassion, but most of them came for selfish reasons of mixed curiosity and pity.

Miriam saw them around her with indifference. Once only she roused herself to cry, "Go, go, there is nothing to see; the child is not dying yet!"

The people who were in the room went away reproved . . .

In the afternoon a carriage stopped at the cottage

door. It was the warden's britzska, and a very old woman was seated in it. As she could not move without assistance, the servants lifted her out carefully, and carried her into the house. It was Sarah Grün, widow of a former warden of the community, and mother of Frau Hanna, whose stories were so deservedly popular in Barnow. Hanna was sixty years of age, and was nicknamed "Babele" (grannie), and Sarah, who was ninety, was called "Urbabele" (great-grandmother). They were known by these names to every one, great and small, Christian and Jewish, in the little town, and their superior age, wisdom, and knowledge were much respected. Miriam had formerly been a servant in their house, and had won the love of the old woman, who, notwithstanding the opposition of her friends, had now come to see her.

She was carried into the room, and put down on a chair. Miriam glanced indifferently toward her, then seeing who she was, her eyes brightened. "Urbabele!" she cried, throwing herself at the feet of the old woman—"Urbabele, God bless you! . . .

She could not say more. Sobs stifled her voice, for at last she wept. The old woman passed her hand gently over her bent head. "Do not speak," she said; "I know your trouble—we all know it. . . . Do not speak, but hear what I have to propose; listen quietly. . . ."

Her own tears were flowing, and falling over her pale sweet face as she spoke.

"I do not know—I am an old woman, my feet refuse to carry me, and my head is not as strong as it was—but I believe we are wrong in letting your child die. Yes, very wrong ; for I do not believe it to be God's will that she should die, nor the will of the great rabbi of Sadagóra—since he is inspired by the spirit of God. . . ."

The old woman paused for a moment, shaking her head as if she wished to negative some thought that had risen to her mind. Then she continued :

"Yes, he has certainly done great wonders. God's spirit moves him, and he has spoken His will concerning you and your child. We must believe what he says. I say that, whether we wish or not, we *must* believe him. For if we lose our faith in him, we lose our faith in everything. . . . Therefore our rabbi did not deserve the hard things you said to him yesterday."

"Ah, if you only knew ! . . ."

"Do not speak !" said the old woman, emphatically, as if she wished to impress each word on the widow's mind ; "do not speak, do not excuse yourself. You need no excuse. My God ! who could blame you, when your child's life was at stake ? I can not, for I also am a mother. . . . But listen to me : whatever the rabbi ordains must be—as you know. . . . I have thought of everything, and your only chance is to go to Sadagóra, and beg for the life of your child."

"And leave her alone, when she is ill?" cried Miriam.

"I will do all I can for her," said the old woman ; and the gravedigger's wife added, " I will nurse her as if she were my own child."

"Must I go?" cried the unhappy mother.

"You must," answered the old woman decidedly ; but she added more gently, "at least it seems that you ought to go, but God alone knows what is right. Ah, Miriam, you do not know how much I have thought and suffered for you and your child! For eighty years of my life, I have never lost my faith in God and in His prophets, and now I begin to doubt!"

Then she collected herself, and said in a tone of command : "Miriam, you *must* go to the rabbi. To-morrow morning early, Simon the carrier is going to start for Czernowitz, with two women. He will take you as far as Sadagóra. I will engage your seat for you in the cart ; and here is money for going and re-turning. In three days you can be home again, and I am convinced you will find Lea getting better. Will you go, Miriam? It concerns the whole town—but that is nothing to you—it concerns your child that you should go."

The poor woman had a hard struggle. Her old

belief in God had been without avail, for the child was growing weaker. As a drowning man catches at a straw, she determined to beseech forbearance from the man whom she had cursed.

"I will go," she said, with a sort of agony.

.   .   .   .

And she did go.

Next morning she started with Simon and the two women, passing out of the town, and along the high-road which leads southward into Bukowina. What she suffered in taking leave of her child shall not be here described; there is enough that is sad in my story.

The sun was rising. It was a cold, dull September sun, and it shone with a pale light upon the flat desolate country, and upon the cart which crawled slowly along the muddy highroad. The clouds were gathering like a thick veil, and the day became more and more dull as the clouds grew heavier.

The soft, mild autumn wind sighed across the plain, and at times a gust shook the canvas awning of the cart.

The horses made their way slowly along the broad neglected road, beneath the leafless dripping trees, and past mist-enshrouded pools and poor villages, which looked doubly miserable on this miserable day. In many places the road was axle-deep in mud, so that the cart stuck fast. Simon and the three women had to dismount and push, in order to get it under way again. Miriam was certainly the weakest of the party, but she worked the hardest. She only roused herself at these times. Generally she sat with closed eyes, as if asleep.

She went through terrible suffering. Her eyes were shut, but vivid pictures were continually before them. She thought she saw her child stretching out her little arms toward her. Some one seemed to bend over the little girl. Was it the gravedigger's wife? No, it was not she, it was a white-robed figure, with a pale bloodless countenance, like the Angel of Death. . . .

Another moment she imagined she was in the presence of the great rabbi of Sadagóra. He looked stern and hard, but she entreated him earnestly, as only a mother can entreat, for the life of her child, and he drove her away with cruel words. She thought she came back and found her child dead ! . . . And again she pictured to herself that he received her kindly, saying, "Your child shall live," and she came home and found Lea dead . . . dead ! . . .

It was frightful ! . . . The mild autumn wind still blew across the heath ; but was it only the plaintive sound of the wind that reached her ears ? When it blew a little stronger she thought it sounded like Lea's voice, crying, "Mother ! . . . Mother ! . . ."

"Did you hear anything ?" cried Miriam wildly, seizing the hand of the woman nearest her. . . .

At about two o'clock in the afternoon the cart stopped at a large, lonely tavern by the roadside, between Thuste and Zalesczyki. The horses were to rest here before proceeding farther. A well-appointed traveling carriage, out of which the horses had been taken, stood at the door, bespattered with mud as though from a long journey.

"Miriam, we are to stop here for two hours," said the carrier.

The women added compassionately, "Come, Miriam, get out. You will be ill if you don't eat some warm food."

Miriam got out of the cart and followed them into the large public room. "I must not let myself become ill," she murmured half aloud.

The large room, with its gray damp walls and uneven floor, was almost empty. One little table alone was occupied. The people seated there were a young couple in comfortable traveling attire. The man appeared to be about thirty years of age. He had light hair, and his expression was good-natured and energetic. His companion was a dark-complexioned and beautiful woman, whose bright eyes sparkled in her happy, pleasant face. That they were newly married was evident, and they talked and laughed and joked as they ate. They were enjoying but a poor meal, consisting of bread and eggs, for they had considered the prices of the tavern extortionate.

The three women sat down in a corner. "That is our Frau Gräfin's head forester," whispered one woman to the other; "he has just married a young wife in Czernowitz, and now he must be bringing her home to Barnow."

"To Barnow?" asked Miriam hastily; but she sank back in her chair again—she had to go to Sadagóra.

The women ordered refreshment, and Miriam ate a mouthful or two. She soon pushed her plate away, and when Simon came into the room, went up to him, and asked, "Must we stay here so long?"

"Yes—because of the horses," he answered. "We must stop here until four o'clock."

"So long!" she sighed. "How many miles are we from Barnow!"

"Only three miles.* The road is so bad."

"Only three miles!" she reiterated with dismay. "When shall we arrive at Sadagóra?"

"The day after to-morrow, at noon."

"The day after to-morrow!" she cried. "Then I can not be at home for six days, and the Sabbath as well! Seven days—that is a whole week! Oh my God! my God!"

She sat down in her corner again, and pressed her hands to her face. But she could not shut out the pictures that had haunted her on the way.

* An Austrian mile is equal to 4·714 English miles.

Again it seemed that she heard the feeble cry of "Mother! . . . Mother!" coming through the walls.

The travelers had overheard her conversation with the carrier, and when they saw the woman's despair, asked him what was wrong.

Simon raised his hat respectfully to the gentle-folks, and related Miriam's story.

When he had finished, the husband and wife looked at one another.

"It is dreadful, is it not, Ludmilla?" said the forester. "What a horrible superstition! . . .

"It is horrible, Karl," answered she. The happy expression left her face, and she looked at Miriam with the deepest compassion.

The poor woman still sat motionless with her hands pressed upon her face. She was shaken with physical pain and feverishness; but the storm within her breast was infinitely greater.

The forester paid his bill, and his coachman came and announced that the carriage was ready. The travelers put on their overcoats, but they did not seem in a hurry to start.

"Karl," said the young wife, undecidedly.

"What do you wish, Ludmilla?"

"Karl—the poor, poor woman! . . ."

"Yes, Ludmilla, she is very much to be pitied. . . ." They again paused on their way to the door.

Miriam at the same moment let her hands fall,

after passing them over her face, as if to clear her thoughts. Seeing the travelers ready to go, she rose and came toward them.

She looked at the lady with endless petition in her eyes, and folded her hands as if in prayer to God, but she could not utter a word.

The lady's eyes filled with tears as she gazed at the pale grief-stricken face before her. "Can I help you?" she asked.

"To Barnow," stammered Miriam. "Can you take me to Barnow?"

"Willingly," answered the lady. "We shall be glad to take you—shall we not, Karl?"

"Ah, yes," he answered.

"And the rabbi!" screamed the two Jewish women. "Are you not going to the rabbi?"

"What will the community say?" objected the carrier.

"They may say what they like," she answered— "I must go to my child!"

She seemed to lose her strength again after this effort, and the gentleman and his servant had almost to carry her to the carriage. They placed her beside the lady, and the forester took the opposite seat. Poor Miriam did not observe this, and did not thank him. "Drive as fast as the horses can go," he said to the coachman, and then she looked at him gratefully.

She sat silently beside her newly found friends, only now and then moving restlessly, as if the pace was too slow.

The horses went quickly, and it was still daylight when they reached Barnow. The people in the streets stared at the ill-assorted company in the carriage, and put their heads together as to what it could mean.

The lady blushed, but her husband shook his head, and said, "What does it matter to us?" When they passed the large figure of the Virgin which stands in a niche of the monastery wall, a sudden thought occurred to him, and he said softly to his wife: "She was called Miriam (Mary), and was a poor Jewish woman, and her heart was torn with grief for her child!"

It was dark when they stopped at the door of the little cottage by the graveyard.

Miriam sprang quickly out of the carriage. "May God reward you!" she breathlessly ejaculated.

"Have you a doctor?" asked the gentleman.

"No," she replied; "the doctor is away, passing the recruits."

"Then I will send the private physician from the castle to see you," he shouted.

Miriam, however, was beyond hearing, as she had hastened into the house.

The sick child was alone. A lamp threw its light

upon her flushed face, and showed that her skin was covered with moisture. She had only a light sheet thrown over her.

Miriam quickly put warm blankets on the bed. "Her skin is moist," she thought joyfully—"that is a sign of recovery."

Almost immediately, the gravedigger's wife returned to her charge. She was much surprised to see Miriam, but she did not venture to reproach her for coming back.

"The child was in such a heat," was all she said, "that I took off all the blankets."

"That was a mistake," answered Miriam; "it is wrong to check perspiration."

Then she knelt by the bed, feeling as if all must now go well.

An hour later a carriage stopped at the door. It brought the private physician from the castle.

He examined the child, felt her pulse, and then covered her carefully again; after which he desired the women to give him an account of the illness from beginning to end.

"She has been in great danger," he said, when they had concluded, "but that is over now. It was most fortunate that you were aware of the necessity of keeping her warm when perspiration began."

Miriam's eyes glistened. "And if we had not been so?" she asked.

The doctor looked at her with surprise. "What a strange question! . . ." he said.

"Answer me, I entreat!" she cried.

"Well," he replied, hastily, "the child would certainly, or rather, would probably, have died."

"God be praised!" cried Miriam, adding, as she turned proudly to her companion, "Now will you say that God has cursed me, when He has worked such a miracle for me? It *was* a miracle that the kind gentlefolks arrived at the tavern at the same time as I— it *was* a miracle, for otherwise my child would have died!"

The child recovered.

And what did the people of Barnow say?

The conviction that a mother's love is strong enough to conquer ill-will, and bring healing and salvation, would not have made them cease their rancor toward the widow and her child; but this, in their eyes, was a visible miracle wrought by God, and such a miracle was of course more powerful than even a decree of the wonder-working rabbi.

ESTERKA REGINA.

(1872.)

ESTERKA REGINA.

Esterka Regina! . . .

That was what we schoolboys used to call her when we returned home for the midsummer holidays from the gymnasium at Taropol, or from that at Czernowitz; and later on, when we were students at the University of Vienna, we called her by the same name whenever we talked of the girls at Barnow during any of our meetings with each other. Her real name was Rachel Welt, and afterward, when she married lanky Chaim, the cattle-dealer, Rachel Pinkus. She was a poor girl who lived in the Jewish quarter in Barnow. She lived in the small dwelling close to the Jewish slaughter-house, and her father, Hirsch Welt, was a butcher. He was a big burly man, and was disliked because of his rough ways.

But that did not prevent us admiring her from a distance, and the Christian *élégants* of Barnow did the same with less reserve than we. The unmarried members of the provincial court, instead of walking in

the Graf's garden during their leisure hours—a place
where they would have enjoyed plenty of fresh air
and the perfume of flowers—chose rather to wander up
and down the narrow street in front of the slaughter-
house, where but little fresh air and no aromatic odors
were to be found. Even the officers of the garrison
never seemed to tire of watching Hirsch Welt as he
used his butcher's knife in strict accordance with Talmudic law. One and all of these loungers were actu-
ated by the desire to catch a glance from the bright
eyes of Esterka Regina ! . . .

It was a name that suited her exactly, and there
was nothing exaggerated in it, although a poet had
given it her. This poet was Herr Thaddäus Wiliszewski. He had studied philosophy in Lemberg, but
unfortunately had been unable to pass his examination—a hopeful youth, who always wore a tightly
buttoned Czamara and long hair, and who wrote
verses, either for home use or for the Krakau "Ladies'
Journal." The first time that Herr Thaddäus saw
Rachel Welt walking by the river in her poor Sabbath
frock, he exclaimed in delight, "Now I understand the
Bible at last ! Esther must have looked like that when
the King of Persia turned away his face and ordered
that Haman should die on the gallows ; and so must
that other Esther, who induced our good King Kazi-
mirz, the peasant's friend, to allow the Jews to settle
freely in Poland, after the wise Germans had turned

them out. She is Esterka, the queen!" And from that time forward all the educated people in Barnow called her nothing but Esterka Regina.

I repeat that there was no exaggeration in this name. Perhaps I had better content myself with making this assertion. For were I to add that her eyes were deep, dark, and bright as the sea on a starlight night, that her hair was black and perfumed like a southern night, and that her smile resembled a dream of spring—you would even then have no clearer idea of her beauty. I knew her, and remember her well. But the thought of that lovely creature fills my heart with sorrow. Her beauty was anything but a blessing to the dear child—nay, it was perhaps a curse. Beautiful, queenly Esterka was very unhappy.

She is so no longer, nor has she been so for many years. She is happy now. She is sleeping in the "good place." They laid her there to rest in peace one spring day long years ago.

May her sleep be calm and sweet, for she suffered much, and her sorrow was even greater than her beauty. The cause of her death was entered in the register as heart complaint, and truly so, for she died of a broken heart.

A most unusual thing to die of—far more unusual than any one thinks. Very few people die of it, and those who most loudly bewail their misery, and say that they are sure to die of a broken heart, generally live a long time, and at last die of old age or indigestion.

Rachel never complained of her lot by word or sigh. She went about the house as usual, and did her work as long as she could. When her strength failed her, and she knew that her end was at hand, she sat down tremblingly and wrote a long letter in the Hebrew character, sealed it, and then tottered out to the post-office with it. She asked the clerk to write the address for her in German: "An den wohlgebórenen Herrn Dr. Adolph Leiblinger, holländischen Stabsartz in Batavia." The young man smiled when she dictated this address to him, but on glancing at her face and seeing that the hand of death was upon her, his smile died away. She got a receipt for the letter which she registered, and then tottered home and died.

Hers was a very simple story—simple as all the stories one meets with in real life, which differ from those thought out in a poet's brain—inasmuch as life is the greatest and most unrelenting of poets. When I attempt to transcribe the events of this story, I can not remain calm and unmoved, for I knew beautiful, unhappy Esterka Regina! . . .

I knew her when she was a little girl of seven years old, and I was a mischievous boy, grumbling at the strict discipline of school. I used to see her every day at that time. When I ran down the gloomy little street on cold winter mornings with

my satchel of books on my back, I was in the habit
of stopping at the door of the house in which she
lived, and calling out "Aaron! Aaron!" for one of
my school-fellows — black Aaron — lived in a poor
garret of the same house with his mother. Hirsch
Welt had given the use of this room out of charity
to Chane Leiblinger, who was the widow of a butcher's
man ; for she was very poor, and could scarcely keep
herself and her boy from starving by the exercise
of her trade of fruit-seller. The moment I had
called Aaron, the door opened very softly, and little
Rachel came out, her hands hidden under her pinafore. Then the poor boy came down the worm-eaten
wooden stairs, dressed in threadbare clothing, and
Rachel hastily thrust the food she had been hiding
in her pinafore into his hand.

He took it, often with hesitation, and always without a word of thanks ; but he would look at the child
strangely and smile. No one who had not seen it
could have believed that that grave, stern-looking
boy could smile, and smile so kindly too ! . . .

"Aaron, will you come with me to the ice? I am
going to slide."

"No."

"Why not? You're always so quiet, and your
eyes look so gloomy !"

"What reason have I to be happy? Is poverty
such a cheering thing? Cold is very disagreeable,

and so is hunger. Or is it the blows I have to endure that should make me happy? The schoolmaster
beats me, and so do all the Christian boys; and why?
Because we crucified *Him?* *I* didn't crucify Him.
Why do they beat me?"

"Oh, it'll be all right when we're grown up and
are barristers."

"I shall never be a barrister; I intend to be a
very great and very rich doctor. Then I shall come
back to Barnow and say to old Hirsch, 'Here are a
hundred ducats, which will pay off all our arrears of
rent.' After that, the Poles will come to me and
entreat me to cure their diseases and to lend them
money; but I shall turn upon them and say, 'Go
away, you dogs!'"

"And Rachel?"

"What's that to you? Well—if you really want
to know—I intend to marry Rachel, and when she is
my wife she shall wear silk gowns; but they must
be a thousand times more splendid than those that
the Gräfin . . ."

Aaron Leiblinger was strange and somewhat eccentric even as a boy. There was nothing very notice-
able in his appearance: he was short and insignifi-
cant-looking, and his face was almost ugly, but it
was redeemed by beautiful and expressive eyes. His
forehead was low, and the hair that hung over it was
black and curly. He was of a thoughtful disposition,

and many of his ideas were surprising in a boy who was the son of an ignorant hawker, and who lived in a miserable garret. He made, or rather forced, his way through life by his quick intelligence, firmness, and energy. For a time it might have been said of him that he succeeded in all his aims and desires. His mother had intended him to help her in her labors as fruit-seller as soon as he had learned to read the Prayer-book; but Aaron wanted to go to a Thorah school, and he went. He wanted to learn the Talmud, and to know it better than his school-fellows, and he succeeded. After that, he wanted to go to the Christian school—an unheard-of thing—and yet he had his own way.

The means he employed were unusual. First of all he told his mother of his determination. The woman was pious and narrow-minded, so she cursed and swore, and then hastened to tell the members of session with loud cries and lamentations that her son intended to become a Christian. For what other reason could induce a Jewish boy to go to a Christian school? The doctor certainly sent his sons to it; but then, the doctor was only half a Jew, and wore a "German" suit of clothes. The chiefs of session praised the woman for her pious zeal, and sent for the boy. He came, and before they could overwhelm him with the remonstrances and threats they deemed suitable for the case, he said: "I know all that you

9

would tell me, so you may save yourselves the trouble of speaking to me. Now, listen to me, for you don't know what I have to say to you. I intend to go to the Christian school, for I am determined to learn everything that can be learned. We need not discuss that point, because my mind is made up. What we have to settle is, whether I am to do it as a Christian or as a Jew. My mother can no longer support me— she is growing old—so I tell you plainly that if you will give me food, clothes, and books, I will remain a Jew, and will teach the children for that remuneration. If you refuse, I shall become a Christian— the fat dean will do anything to secure the salvation of a soul."

This strange and eccentric address was not ineffectual. The elders of the congregation bowed before the iron will of the boy, and gave him the small help that he demanded. He went to the monastery school as a Jew, in caftan and curls. It was dreadful what he suffered in consequence of this dress. Perhaps God counted the tears he shed and the blows he received; he grew tired of counting them, tired of weeping. He bore everything—injustice and blows, hunger and cold, or the few, very few, acts of kindness shown him — with the same gloomy and defiant composure. An unquenchable longing for knowledge and an unquenchable thirst for vengeance sustained him. His face even quite

lost its youthful expression. My schoolfellow, Aaron
Leiblinger, was much, very much, to be pitied.

But even the poorest life possesses some treasure
to which it clings. The gloomy, reserved boy loved
little Rachel dearly. His face softened strangely and
touchingly when he was talking to her. I used to
feel, though I could not have told why, that it did
him good to speak to him about the child. I believe that he would have died for her unhesitatingly.
And once a very curious thing happened—he wept—
when Rachel had small-pox.

He scarcely shed a tear when his mother died.
Her death made no great void in his life, and apparently did not much move him. He lived alone in
the garret now — that was all. Burly old Hirsch
Welt provided him with food after that, but he did
not trespass long on his kindness. One summer
morning he came to see me very early. "Good-by,"
he said; "I've come to say good-by, because you
were always kind to me. I'm going away from Barnow to-day, that I may become a rich man."

"But you'll starve by the way."

"Oh no; I have the money that my mother left
—three florins. I'm going to Lemberg—good-by."

So he went away, and I did not hear of him
again for a long, long time.

Esterka Regina! . . .

It was a summer day—a bright, beautiful afternoon in July. The sun was shining on the heath,
which was sweet with flowers and musical with the
hum of insects. Although a dull solitary place during the greater part of the year, it was full of color,
perfume, and life in summer. All was quiet and
still in the Ghetto; no one was moving about in
the street; the bustle of trade was hushed.

The young people were walking by the river-
side, dressed in their best clothes. The young men
looked pale and old of their age, and their conversation was no more suited to their years than their
appearance. They discussed their Talmudic studies
and their business; it seldom happened that one of
them whispered to his friend that he thought the
girl who had just passed was very pretty, and that
he should esteem himself lucky if his father were to
fix upon her for his bride. It would be hard to say
what the girls talked about. Who can tell what
thoughts fill the head of a Jewish maiden, or why
she titters as she passes down the walk in her best
gown on a fine Sabbath afternoon.

Why? Well, perhaps at the sight of the young
gentlemen who, in spite of their wearing neither
caftan nor curls, came to walk on the "Jewish
promenade" by the river, as if it were a matter of,
course for them to be there. And yet it was an
unusual sight to see them there, for they were

Christians, and grand people; and such do not
generally haunt Jewish resorts. But it was worth
while to make a sacrifice for the chance of seeing
Esterka Regina—even a greater sacrifice than that
of spending an hour or two on the Jewish promenade. The three groups of *élégants* waited patiently, watching the stars of the society—the Re-
beccas, Miriams, and Doras—until at length the sun
appeared—the butcher's beautiful daughter. There
were three groups, I said. There were the military
cadets and lieutenants of the Lichtenstein Hussars, in
their light blue uniforms, led by fair, talkative, little Szilagy; there were young Polish nobles and
literati, with the long-haired poet, Herr Thaddäus
Wiliszewski, at their head; and lastly, there were a
number of boys at home for the holidays, among
whom was a youth, who is no longer a youth now,
and who feels sad at heart whenever he thinks of
that glorious summer afternoon. For its glory has
long since departed, and that lovely girl sank into
her early grave years ago, a broken-hearted woman.

But I can see her now as distinctly as I did on
that day when she came slowly down the lime-tree
walk leaning on the arm of a girl-friend. There
was a stir among all at her approach: even the
Jewish youths felt the influence of her beauty, and
many of them involuntarily straightened their caf-
tans and the long curl at either side of their faces.

The three groups that I mentioned before prepared
for the encounter. The blue-coated hussars took up
the first line as beseemed brave warriors, and fore-
most among them was little Szilagy, for he was the
most audacious. She walked on slowly, and at last
came close to him, he having placed himself directly
in her way. She did not cast down her eyes like
the other girls on passing these would-be lady-killers,
but, on the contrary, held up her head and looked
about her as calmly and indifferently as if the blue-
coated hussars had been nothing but blue mist.
When, however, she was forced to stand still, because the impudent little man had placed himself so
that she could not pass him, her expression changed.
This was clearly shown by Szilagy's conduct : he
flushed as red as a peony, stepped back, and—incredible as it may sound—saluted her awkwardly. When
Herr von Szervay laughed at him afterward for
having been routed with such disorder, he said, " I
have plenty of courage, and have often proved it,
but I couldn't stand the way that she looked at
me. . . ."

The second group, who had witnessed the defeat
of the hussars, thought discretion the better part of
valor, and drew back betimes, the long-haired poet
gazing with great eyes of astonishment and delight at
the beautiful girl who was passing him. It was at that
moment that Herr Thaddäus's poor little brain, which

hitherto had only been capable of making verses for home use or for the Krakau "Ladies' Journal," was suddenly inspired to invent the name that I have put at the head of this story. . . .

And the third group! The schoolboys were neither irresistible nor had they any ambition to appear so ; they had hardly courage to look at the sparkling black eyes of the lesser lights, and when they saw the loveliest of all the Jewish maidens approaching them, they huddled together like a flock of frightened sheep. But one of their number—I can not tell to this day how I found courage to do it—stepped forward boldly and spoke to the girl—a good deal less boldly. . . .

"Pardon me, Fräulein," I stammered, touching my hat, "perhaps you don't remember me—little Aaron. . . ."

"Yes, I remember you," she answered kindly ; "you were always a good friend to him. Have you heard of him lately?"

"No, I haven't heard anything about him since he went away."

"Then I know more than you do. Old Itzig Türkischgelb, the 'Marschallik'—you know the silly old man—was at Lemberg a short time ago, and when there he chanced to meet Aaron, so he stopped and spoke to him. He hardly knew him at first ; for just fancy what our poor little Aaron has become! He has become a gentleman, and dresses and speaks like a German. He left the Latin school three years ago, and ever since then he has lived at Vienna, where he is learning to be a doctor! Who ever would have believed it? And," she added, hesitatingly, "the 'Marschallik' says that he has grown very proud, and will not speak to a Jew. Only think, he calls himself Adolf now, and they say that he is going to become a Christian. I can't believe it, though—can you?"

I would not have believed in the possibility of anything that was disagreeable to the girl for the world.

"No," I answered with decision, "I don't believe it either. However, I shall soon have an opportunity of knowing for certain. I'm going to Vienna in a few weeks, to the university; and when I am there I'll look up Aaron or Adolf, whichever he calls himself."

"Yes, do," she said, quickly. "How glad he will be to see you again! And," she added, her cheeks flushing, "remember me to him if he hasn't forgotten me. But—you understand—only if he hasn't forgotten me. . . ."

"Oh," I exclaimed, boldly and enthusiastically, "who could forget you?"

I was so terrified by my own boldness that I at once touched my hat and withdrew, stammering some words of farewell. But I managed to regain sufficient mastery over myself, before I joined my companions, to be able to receive the storm of curiosity, envy, and admiration with which they greeted me, with dignified calmness.

. . . .

I did not set off in search of Aaron or Adolf Leib-linger as soon as I arrived in Vienna, although I had fully determined to do so. Who will not at once un-derstand the reason? Imagine a lad of eighteen years of age, shy, poor, ignorant of the world, and brought up in a small country town, suddenly removed from all his accustomed surroundings and transplanted to one of the great capitals of Europe. He would naturally feel lost and dazed in the crowd hurrying past him, and among the endless streets and houses stretched out before him. He would need time to grow used to the change in his life, and to gain courage to face it. It was so with me. And then again, how was I to find him among the four thousand students who attended the university classes? I gave up the idea, and trusted to chance.

It was on a dismal afternoon in December that we met at last. There had been a thick mist all day, which after a time became a fine persistent and very wetting rain. It was so disagreeable that I was driven to take refuge in a large crowded *café* in the Alster suburb, in hopes of the shower passing off. Every seat was occupied, but at last I succeeded in finding a vacant chair in the billiard-room. The rain lasted so long that I grew tired of watching the drip from the leaves of the plants in the garden, and turned my attention to the game that was going on.

Three young men were playing at pool. The marker addressed them all as "Herr Doctor," so I saw that they must be medical students. My attention was particularly drawn to one of the three—a slender and rather delicate-looking man of middle height, with marked but finely cut features. He would have looked pale anyhow, but the intense blue-black of his wavy hair and beard made him appear almost startlingly pallid. His face could not be called handsome—his lips were too thin for that, and his forehead too low. The moment I caught sight of his face, I saw that he had a story; it did not occur to me at first that I had ever seen him before. But suddenly, when the thin lips were firmly pressed together, and the low forehead was contracted into a frown at some jesting remark of one of his companions, it flashed upon me all at once—"That is black Aaron!" And so it was. I can hardly tell whether our meeting was a pleasurable one; at any rate, our pleasure was not unmixed. When two young people have been separated for some time, they are apt to be rather shy with each other when they first meet, for they hardly know how much change may have taken place in each other's ways and ideas. This is doubly the case after a long separation, such as Aaron's and mine. We strove hard to bring back the old footing that had existed between us, but in vain. Our conversation was disjointed, and threatened to come to a speedy conclusion, when I suddenly remembered the message with which I had been intrusted.

"Somebody at Barnow," I said, "is very much interested in your career. Can you guess who it is?"

"No." And so saying he blew a cloud of tobacco-smoke nonchalantly in the air. "My dear boy, you have no idea how much trouble I have given myself to forget the people at Barnow, entirely—absolutely."

"Even your guardian angel, little Rachel?"

"What, was it Rachel?" he exclaimed, eagerly. And then resuming his indifferent manner: "What has become of the little girl? She must be pretty big now, though—sixteen years old or thereabout."

"And very beautiful too," I replied.

I then proceeded to give him such an enthusiastic description of her beauty and intelligence, that he could not help smiling. But when I had finished, he said, gravely—"I am very sorry to hear it—very!"

"Why? What do you mean?"

"I am very grateful to the little guardian angel of my boyhood, and should like her to be happy. But there's very small hope of that, if she is really as beautiful and intelligent as you say. She will either be tempted beyond her power of resistance, and fall a prey to some Polish or Hungarian swell in spite of all her wisdom. . . ."

"Impossible !" I cried, indignantly.

"Or else she will remain the good obedient child of a father who will one day give her to wife, whether she will or not, to some rude illiterate member of the Chassidim. And as she possesses more intelligence than most women, she will sooner or later feel the whole misery and humiliation of her lot very keenly, and will at length die a poor broken-hearted creature in some corner of a Podolian Ghetto."

"You take too black a view of the subject."

"I see things as they are. You need not tell me what the Chassidim are. Don't let us discuss the matter further. Good-by for the present."

So we parted, and although we spoke of meeting again, our words were cool.

We did not give ourselves any trouble to bring about another meeting. But accident at length brought us together again, and for a longer time.

Early in spring, I moved into new lodgings, and the first time that I looked out at my window, I saw the face of my old schoolfellow at Barnow, in an opposite window, side by side with that of the skeleton he was studying. He lived in the same house and in the same quadrangle as I did. We therefore renewed our acquaintance in some measure, and gradually even became friends—that is to say, as far as it was possible for students of such different standing (he was in his fourth year, I only in my first), and for characters so dissimilar as ours, to be friends.

As regards his character, one saw in him a clear proof of the truth of the old saying, that "the impressions of childhood are the most deeply rooted of all." Adolf Lieblinger, student of medicine, was the same in character as black Aaron. The metamorphosis of the reserved ugly boy, into the able, worldly, interesting young man, had left the basis of his character untouched : he still possessed the same defiant spirit and the same consciousness of his own powers, and the same hatred as of old was hidden away at the bottom of his heart. Besides that, he was unchanged in his gratitude for every kindness, however small, and in his thirst after knowledge. When he first left Barnow, he had had a hard struggle for existence, and yet he had passed his examination at the gymnasium in an incredibly short space of time. He made his way both there, and afterward at the University of Vienna. And so he still regarded the old proverb, "Where there's a will there's a way," as essentially true.

He was only changed in one respect ; his ideas of God and religion were fundamentally altered. In the old days, partly because he was so proud, he had clung all the more tenaciously to the religious teach-

ing of his childhood that he had been persecuted for
holding it, and his God had been more or less the
God of his own vengeance ; for he had never tired of
imploring Him to send down a flash of lightning to
destroy the Christian boys who bullied him, and our
stupid, rough-mannered teachers. But now he was
indifferent to God, and hated the Jewish faith with
a bitter hatred. He always spoke of Jews and Judaism with passionate virulence. Herr Thaddäus Wiliszewski, who had written some verses for his friends,
and not for the "Ladies' Journal" this time, which he
called a "Poem against the Jews," was mild as a dove
in comparison. But still he remained in appearance
a member of the old faith. "My coat is uncomfortable," he used to say, " and doesn't fit me well, but
I can't find any other on the face of the earth that
would fit me better ; and, as you know, one can't go
about coatless—people would stare so !"

I grew very fond of Adolf—as fond as I used to
be of Aaron when I was a boy; so when the vaca-
tion approached, I invited him to accompany me to
my eastern home, and was heartily glad when he
accepted my invitation.

During this journey our conversation chanced to
turn on Rachel as we speeded through the night in
the railway toward Barnow. Her name had never
been mentioned by either of us since the day on
which we had first met in Vienna.

"Take care of yourself," I said jestingly; "old love never rusts out."

He laughed. "I," he said, "what have *I* to do with love? You know that love is soft and tender, and I—am a hard man." He laughed again, and then added gravely and almost tenderly: "Look here—I will avoid seeing Rachel. The memory of her is the only pleasurable one of my boyhood, and shall I do well to destroy it by going to see her? for doubtless she is now a shy and dirty girl who would address me in Jewish-German."

He opened the carriage-window and stared out into the dark night for many minutes.

.   .   .   .

We arrived at Barnow at the end of July. "Black Aaron's" coming awakened great excitement, and it was both ludicrous and sad to see the way in which the orthodox Jews received him. He, "black Aaron," Aaron Leiblinger, son of Chane Leiblinger, who used to live in the cottage by the river, actually dared to wear "Christian" clothes, to eat "Christian" food, to smoke on the Sabbath; and had even gone so far as to study! Deadly sins all of these in the eyes of the orthodox,—sins that should meet with condign punishment! No one spoke to him, and any one he addressed turned away from him in scorn. The little boys ran after him in the street, shouting, *Meschumed!* (apostate). The young man laughed at the children, and repaid the scorn of their elders in the same coin. We did not often put ourselves in the way of these people, however, but used to make long expeditions into the country, and visited the Christian officials of the town. We were heartily welcomed by the latter. Herr Thaddäus Wiliszewski was kind enough to read his poems to us, and the sallow daughters of the Steueramts-Vorsteher * allowed us to flirt with them a little. Adolf was outwardly full of laughter and fun, and I alone guessed how bitterly he felt the reception he had met with from his own people. He kept true to his determination not to see Rachel.

One day—it was on a fearfully hot Sunday afternoon in August, the second we had spent in the little town—the tempter came to him at last, or rather, came to me in the first instance. I was alone at home that afternoon, when the door opened, and a little manikin, with a very red nose and very thin legs, trotted into the room. It was Herr Isaak Türkischgelb, the "Marschallik" of Barnow, which, being interpreted, means the merrymaker, or marshal of weddings at Barnow. A dignitary of this kind, besides a thousand other duties, is intrusted with that of inviting the guests to a marriage. It was in this capacity that he honored me with a visit. He had been sent by Frau Sprinze Klein to invite Adolf

---

* Head of the office for the assessment of taxes.

and me to the wedding-party, to be given on the following Tuesday in honor of the marriage of her daughter, Jutta Klein, to Herr Isidor Spitz (*vulgo*, "Red Itzigel").

"Thank you," I said. "But shall we see any pretty girls there? Is Esterka Regina to be one of the guests?"

"Who?" asked the little man in amazement, putting his hand up to his ear and bending forward the better to hear my answer.

"Well, I mean Rachel Welt, the fat butcher's daughter."

"Do you ask if she is to be there?" cried the Marschallik, pathetically. "Is it reasonable to suppose that any one would invite all the ugly girls in Barnow and leave out the most beautiful? Take my word for it, young sir, Sprinze Klein and I know how to act on such occasions; and it is an acknowledged thing that when you invite young men to a party, you ought to have some pretty girls to meet them. Besides that, we know that we needn't deck out a room with flowers when Rachel is there, for she is the loveliest flower I ever saw; and that's as true as that God blesses my undertakings!

"The loveliest flower," he repeated; "and so you will come, won't you?—you and your friend Aaron-leben—pardon me for calling him that; for how can I call him Adolf, when I often had him in my arms when he was a little child, and his mother, Chane, was my own sister's daughter? You'll come now, and prevent the people in Barnow saying of the old Marschallik—'He's only fit to invite common Jews, the uneducated folk of the town; he's no good at all where young gentlemen are concerned!'"

I could not help laughing. "All right," I said, "make your mind easy as regards me. But whether Adolf will go or not is a different question; I don't think he will. However, you'd better come back tomorrow and hear what he says."

The little man once more raised his hands in the air, bowing low at the same time; after which, he trotted out of the room with a broad smile upon his face.

I was convinced that I should have to go alone. And, indeed, when I told Adolf of the invitation, he answered testily: "Say no more. I'll follow you to hell if you like, but not to these people!"

"What a pity!" I said. "It would have been such a good opportunity for you to have made an interesting study of the character of—our hostess, Frau Sprinze Klein. You don't know her. She was born at Brzezan, and is now a very rich widow. She keeps a haberdasher's shop."

"Very interesting," he replied, scornfully.

"More so than you imagine. A very grave psychological process is going on in that woman.

She is struggling with all her might to free herself
from the oppressive bonds of orthodoxy, and to
gain a more enlarged view of life; but it must be
confessed that her efforts to attain this end are
very comical, to say the least of it. Frau Klein
lives like every other Jewess. She does not venture to wear her own hair, and can not bring herself to disobey the Levitical laws regarding food
in the smallest particular. But as she once spent
six months in Lemberg when she was a girl, she
has a sort of Platonic love for 'culture' and 'enlightenment.' She begins nearly every sentence with,
'When I was in Lemberg.' She shows her Platonic
love of enlightenment in strange ways. For instance,
she delights in speaking High-German, and whenever she manages to pick up a foreign word, she
continually drags it into her conversation by hook
or by crook for the next week. You may easily
imagine how the unfortunate foreign word suffers
at her hands; or rather, I should say, you can't
imagine it, for it far exceeds the bounds of the
wildest imagination. Here is another example: Frau
Sprinze can't read a word of German, and yet she
bought three second-hand books at a sale—these
are, Schiller's 'Robbers,' a story by Caroline Pich-
ler, and a volume of 'Casanova.' She is in the
habit of keeping one of these books lying open
before her on the counter, and whenever she thinks

that any one is looking at her, she stares at the mysterious characters printed on the page as attentively as though she understood what they meant. If any pious Jew tells her that reading a German book is a deadly sin, she invariably answers: 'When I was in Lemberg, I noticed that the daughters of the chief rabbi were in the habit of reading German books.' At the same she secretly comforts herself by the thought: 'If reading these books is really a sin, I am innocent of committing it. . . .' As a last example of her large-mindedness, we have the invitation to her daughter's marriage-feast. You must know that she has arranged that the dancing at her party shall not be conducted after the 'Jewish fashion'—the men with men and the women with women—but after that of the Christians, which allows men and women to dance with each other. We probably owe the heartiness of our invitation to the fact that very few of the young men who are to be there know how to dance properly."

"How flattering !"

"Pooh ! What does that matter ? It'll be capital fun, I expect ! Even if they only have slow country-dances, I think that the chance of having such a pretty girl as Esterka Regina as a partner would make up for anything. Don't you ?"

"No, I don't," answered Adolf, shortly.

But he looked thoughtful when he heard her name, and next day when the Marschallik came to invite him to Frau Klein's party, he at once consented to go, very much to my surprise and to that of the old man.

. . . On the following Tuesday evening he went to the rich widow's house, which we found grandly decorated for the evening's entertainment. The marriage ceremony had been performed, so that every one was waiting for the dancing to begin. Our hostess met us at the ball-room door and received us more than graciously. She wore a dress of heavy yellow silk, and above that a pale-green velvet mantle; and the well-assorted jeweler's shop (for that is the only way to describe it) that she had hung about her, rattled with every movement she made.

"You will find everything arranged as it is done at Lemberg," she said to us, with a beaming smile; "for when I was at Lemberg, I learned the proper way to do *les horreurs* as hostess!"

We went into the dancing-room. The men did not look enchanted to see us, but the girls seemed to witness our arrival with more satisfaction. We at once set to work to fulfill the duty for which we had come, and danced diligently.

Soon afterward, an old man came into the room accompanied by a young girl. It was Hirsch Welt and his daughter. It was the first time that we had seen her since our return, and, as though with one breath, we ejaculated, "How very beautiful she is!" But I will not even now attempt to describe her.

"Does seeing the girl really destroy the pleasurable memories of your boyhood?" I asked Adolf, with a smile.

But he did not answer. For one moment he turned very pale. Immediately recovering himself, he went up to her and asked her to dance with him.

She also turned pale, looked at him with a startled expression, and answered in a low voice — "No!"

His cheek flushed. "You—you don't dance?"

"I do dance," she replied slowly, and still with the same look in her face, "but not with you."

He forced himself to smile, but with a great effort. "And what have I done to deserve such a punishment?"

"You hate us all, and make game of us—of us, our ways, and our language. And what good does it do you, after all, to act thus? It does not make you the less a Jew."

His face darkened. "Oh, if you only knew," he began hastily, but stopped himself there. After a short pause, he continued, with a smile: "You are mistaken. The people of Barnow have done me no

wrong, nor I them. How could it be otherwise? I
was born and brought up here among them."

"Oh, I know," she said, quickly; "you used to
live in the garret-room in our house, you and your
old mother; peace be with her ! . . ."

His face lighted up with pleasure. "You remember those old days ? I should hardly have expected
it—it's eleven years ago !"

"Yes, I remember it all distinctly. We used to
be great friends, you and I. And had you forgotten
me ?"

"Certainly not !" he said, emphatically.

Then they began to talk in a low voice, and I
could hear no more of their conversation. He was
probably reminding Rachel of a number of little
incidents of their childhood, for a happy smile played
upon her lips every now and then.

Neither of them remembered what a strange thing
it must have seemed to every one present that they
should have so much to say to each other in private.
People began to whisper, and I heard the Platonic
lover of progress say to one of her gossips, 'I saw
may curious things when I was in Lemberg; but I
never knew before that any girl who was engaged to
be married would venture to talk so long to a stranger—I really never did !'"

But at this moment they separated.

"I am so glad that you haven't forgotten old

times," said the girl aloud; "it's a sign that you aren't wicked, though many people say that you are. . . . But now—I must say good-by."

And in another moment she was gone. He gazed after her retreating figure as though in a dream.

I went up to him.

"You've given the unfortunate bridegroom rather a bad half hour," I said, laughingly.

"What!" he asked, quickly, "is she engaged?"

"I heard some one say so just now."

"To whom?"

"I don't know. Didn't she tell you about it?"

"No," he answered, and then begged me to go home—he had had enough of the party.

That was their first meeting.

. . . .

Two months later. The mild autumn sunshine was gilding the landscape, and the heath was brightly tinted with deep russet hues. Adolf and I were once more sitting opposite each other in the railway-carriage, but this time we were going northward, and were leaving Barnow behind us.

Adolf's manner had been rather strange of late. He had sometimes been unreasonably full of high spirits, and again absolutely silent, not a word to be got out of him on any subject; sometimes confident, and again sentimental. Any one could see that the poor fellow was over head and ears in love, and

therefore in a very unsettled frame of mind. I did
not know how matters stood between him and the
girl he loved, and did not care to ask; but I rejoiced
in silence that the spring-time of joy had at last come
to the sad solitary heart of my old friend.

He was very gentle during the whole of that day,
and did not give utterance to a single sarcastic speech.
His face looked softer and brighter than I could have
imagined it possible for those sharply-cut features to
look.

At last he addressed me suddenly.

"I've got something to tell you that you'll be glad
to hear."

"Go on."

But he grew silent again. After a long pause he
burst out all at once: "I love her; she loves me. I
can not bear to keep it to myself any longer, so I will
tell you how it all happened. . . ."

I shook him warmly by the hand, and then he
went on:

"You remember that marriage. I am not a poet,
nor do I find it easy to put my impressions into
words, therefore I simply can not tell you what effect
seeing that girl had upon me, for it was unspeakable,
indescribable. Still, although her dear face was continually before me in imagination, I could not make
up my mind to visit her in her father's house, for
that house was haunted by the ghosts of my miser-

10

able childhood—ghosts I dared not waken without pressing necessity. Besides that, Hirsch Welt is one of the most narrow-minded of the pious sect in the community, and I felt no desire to receive any more proofs of the affection of that lot than I have already had.

"So I left our next meeting to be brought about by chance; and, as chance would have it, I met Rachel again before another week had passed. It was in a curious place—the very last that I should have thought of.

"You know the old ruined castle on the left bank of the Lered; you know it better than I do. I never had any liking for the place, for a love of romantic scenery has no part in my composition; but somehow or other I was that day impelled to climb the hillock on which the ruins lie, after having wandered aimlessly about the heath for hours. I felt—laugh at me if you like—that I must go to the top of some eminence and get a good view of the country round.

"Well, as I said before, I climbed the little hill, and there I found Rachel sitting on a stone in the ruined court, right under the great red wooden cross, the presence of which makes the Jews so averse to visiting the place. She was sewing diligently, and a book was lying on the grass at her side.

"On hearing the sound of my footsteps, she looked up, and returned my greeting quietly.

"'Here you are at last,' she said.

"I stared at her in astonishment. 'Did you know that I was coming? I only came up here by chance.'

"'No one told me that you were coming,' she answered, blushing deeply as she spoke, 'but I was quite sure that you would come. Yes; I brought that book to show you.' She put it in my hand. 'Do you remember it?'

"I remembered it well. A strange feeling came over me as I gazed at the dog's-eared discolored pages. It was a prayer-book, written in Jewish-German for the use of women, and was one of the few things that I had inherited from my mother. In spite of all my hardness, I was profoundly moved— I scarcely knew why.

"My eyes were dim, and I returned the book in silence.

"'You gave it to me,' she said, 'when you went away out into the wide world to seek your fortune on that beautiful summer morning long ago. We cried a great deal when you left us, fair-haired Chaim and I. It is to him that I am engaged, you know. . . .'

"'To him!' I repeated, as calmly as I could. 'You said nothing about your engagement the other evening.'

"'Because we were talking of other things,' she

answered; and then added, 'Nor did you tell me about the girl that you're engaged to, and yet they say that she is very beautiful and grand.'

"I could not help laughing. 'No, Fräulein * Rachel,' I said, 'I'm not engaged.'

"She looked at me questioningly. 'Aren't you? It's another lie, then. Our people say that you're engaged to a very rich and beautiful Christian girl; but,' she continued, speaking quickly and eagerly, 'it's your own fault that they tell so many false and wicked tales about you. You are proud and reserved to all our people, and turn us into ridicule whenever you can. That was the reason why I was so angry with you when I first saw you at the marriage. I soon saw that you weren't wicked, and told you so; but you're proud—even to me.'

"I would have spoken, but she interrupted me.

"'You are; you needn't say no, for it's quite true. Why do you address me so stiffly, and not as you used to do?'

"'Because little Rachel is now a grown-up young lady—'

"'There you are—sarcastic again,' she interrupted, passionately. 'I'm not a young lady—I am only a Jewish girl; so let me beg of you to call me simply by my name, as an old friend should do.'

---

* I have made use of the word "Fräulein" in order to avoid the discussion as to "thou" and "you."—*Translator's note.*

"'Willingly,' I replied; 'but you must do the same by me.'

"'No,' she said, blushing, but with great decision; 'that wouldn't do at all. You are a learned man, and will soon be a doctor, while I—I am only Rachel Welt. You must not ask that of me.'

"We talked," continued Adolf, "for a long time and about many things—not only on that morning, but on many mornings for a number of weeks. Rachel took her work to the ruined castle every day. 'It's so airless down below,' she said; 'and here one can see the sunshine, and the birds that are singing all around. I like plenty of light.' You know how poverty, oppression, and sorrow have stifled almost all sense of the picturesque in the Podolian Jews, but that simple girlish spirit is full of it.

"I was quite as punctual as Rachel in arriving at our meeting-place. Even if I wished, I couldn't tell you all the things we talked about — the smallest matters were weighty enough to us to become the theme of endless conversation. Neither of us knew what it was that drew us to meet so often. It was a happy time we spent together, ignorant of the cause of our joy; perhaps, when I look back at it, it seems almost the brightest part of those bright days. . . ."

Aldolf paused abruptly, and again that look of

softened happiness that I had before remarked passed over his face.

"You are right," I said; "the happiest time of first love is when neither of the lovers has as yet awakened to the cause that makes the most wonderful event seem simple, and the simplest a wonder. It is generally to some external influence that the lovers owe the discovery of how deep this feeling has grown."

Adolf laughed. "You speak like a book," he answered. "But—you're right all the same. The 'external influence,' as you call it, was not wanting in our case."

Then he continued :

"One morning I went to the ruins as usual, but she did not come. Hour after hour I paced the courtyard impatiently, every now and then going to look down the pathway leading to the town. All in vain. Rachel did not come. My disappointment opened my eyes to the fact that she had grown very dear to me.

"She did not appear on the next day or the next. A week passed, and she did not come. I was in despair.

"At last I found her seated in the old place one morning when I went to the castle. I hastened to her and took her hand in mine. 'Thank God! you've come back,' I cried, joyfully. 'Rachel, Rachel, you don't know how anxious I have been about you.'

"She smiled sadly; her face was pale, and her eyelids reddened with weeping. 'I could not come,' she said softly, 'I was ill.'

"'Ill!' I exclaimed. 'And I not with you! I had then good reason to be anxious about you.'

"'It wasn't much,' she returned. 'And you came here often?'

"'Every day—and waited and waited!'

"'Thank you,' she said in a low voice, and held out her hand once more to me.

"As we stood there silent, looking at each other and finding no word to say, we all at once became clearly conscious of our love for each other. We both trembled.

"'I must go,' she said at length, withdrawing her hand from mine. 'My mother will be anxious — good-by.'

"'Till to-morrow,' I answered. 'You will come?'

"'I will come,' she said in a low voice. . . .

"I had not long to wait for her on the following day: she was very punctual.

"I went to meet her shyly, and rather ill at ease, —not joyously, as on the previous day.

"She was still very pale, and showed her weakness by the tremulousness of her walk.

"'You are worse than you'd have me believe,' I said.

"'No,' she replied, 'I am not ill, and'—she

hesitated, and then resumed in a firmer voice—'I haven't been ill. I lied to you yesterday.'

I stared at her in amazement.

"'Yes,' she repeated, 'I lied, because I had not courage to tell the truth. I am pale, and my eyes are red, because I wept so much, and was so miserable during the last week. I've a great deal to say to you, and entreat of you to listen to me quietly.'

"We seated ourselves on the great stone at the foot of the red cross.

"'I don't know,' she began in a clear firm voice, 'who told my parents that I was in the habit of meeting you here every day, and it doesn't much matter who it was. I should have been certain to have told them myself some time, for I saw no harm in what I had done. But one day lately, when I went home, my father received me with vehement reproaches, and with words . . . with words. . . . I will not repeat them, for they were very cruel and unjust. He said that I had forgotten my honor and my duty; he reminded me of the man to whom I am betrothed, and besought me to beware of you, for you were an unbeliever, and would tempt me to evil. His anger did not frighten me, but that did; for something all at once seemed to tell me why I had gone so regularly to the ruins, and why your words and looks made me so happy. Now—I know the truth. And when my father entreated me not to shame him, and to swear a holy oath that I would neither see nor speak to you again, I could not do it. If God and all the angels in heaven had commanded me to take that oath, I couldn't have done it — it would have seemed desecration. I bore my father's anger and my mother's tears, because I knew that I . . . that I loved you. . . .'

"I would have spoken, but she raised her hand to stay me, and continued: .

"'When I first knew the truth I was filled with horror — I could not understand myself; and yet in spite of all that I felt happy. I saw the grief and despair that my conduct brought upon my parents, but, even to please them, I could not remain engaged to Chaim. The world still believes that I am, but I really belong to you. That is the reason why I could not help coming to see you yesterday in secret. Then I saw both in your words and looks that you loved me as really as I loved you. And now I ask you what is to be done? what is to be the end of all this?'

"I did not hear the sadness of every tone of her voice, because I would not hear it—my heart was so full of joy unspeakable.

"'Child,' I cried, 'you love me; then all is well!'

"But she only looked at me gravely and sadly, and after a short pause went on:

"'No — all is lost! . . . You feel happy, and so do I; but while you're contented with that, I look to the future. And there is no comfort, no light to be found there for me. I can not be your wife—the life I have hitherto led has unfitted me for that. I have had no education, no teaching. God knows that I am nothing, know nothing, and can do nothing. Woe is me, I can not even speak "German." What should you, who are going to be a doctor, do with a wife who is utterly ignorant of the life you lead and its ways? Oh, I fear your world with a deadly fear. Were I to marry you and then bring you to shame before others, because of my ignorance and mistakes, you would say in your heart that your love for me had been your bane. . . .'

"'Rachel,' I cried, 'don't say that; you only make both yourself and me miserable by giving way to such idle fears.'

"'I am only saying what is true,' she answered, with trembling lips. 'And then—can I buy my own happiness at the expense of my parents' sorrow?—as our people would regard it—shame? Were I to do so they would die of grief. Often in my misery I felt that I must entreat you to go away—at once. To forget me—would not bring happiness, but safety.'

"'And do you really think that I could forget you?' I asked, gravely. 'Could you forget me?'

"'No,' she said, 'I could not. But tell me—can you see a way out of all this misery?'

"'Yes,' I answered, with determination, for the spirit of defiance was roused within me, and I felt more than ever convinced of the truth of the proverb, 'Where there's a will there's a way.' 'I will go and speak to your father, and prove to him how foolish the prejudice he feels toward me really is. I will entreat him not to make his only child unhappy, and ask him to give you to me. If he will not consent, I will win you by my own labor; but when I have done that, you must leave your parents for your husband. We should have to wait and work for two years. But you will not tire any more than I shall. And then you will be my dear wife, and will be able to look back at your cares and anxieties of to-day with a smile. I swear that you shall be my wife—or else, I shall never marry.'

"'I will be true to you,' she said, in a low voice, but so earnestly that it almost seemed like a sacred oath.

"So we parted. . . ."

Adolf was silent for a time. We stared out into the dusk without speaking, and gazed at the shadowy outlines of the vast plain of Western Galicia.

It was not until the silence had lasted a long time that I asked, "Did you go to Hirsch Welt?"

"Yes," he answered.

"And were you successful?"

"He turned me out of the house," returned Adolf

calmly; "but what of that? Rachel shall be my wife. 'Where there's a will, there's a way!' . . ."

. . . .

Fifteen months passed away after our conversation in the railway-carriage without any event worthy of record taking place. When we returned to Vienna we took up our abode in different parts of the town, and in consequence met but seldom. I only knew that Adolf was working very hard, and that he had good accounts of Rachel.

Early one morning in December, before the sun was well up, I heard a violent knocking at my door, and ere I could call out "Come in," the door opened, and my friend entered hurriedly, his face deadly pale and anxious-looking.

"What! it's you, Adolf!" I exclaimed. "But what's the matter? . . . Is anything wrong?"

He passed his hand across his forehead, and pushed back his hair to which a few snow-flakes were sticking. "I don't know what has happened," he said, "that is the reason I am so uneasy. . . . Don't question me, but get up and come with me. . . ."

I obeyed, and dressed as quickly as I could, for something in his voice and manner made me feel very anxious. He went to the window, and throwing himself into my arm-chair with a weary sigh, stared out into the cold, gray, winter morning. His face was deadly pale, and his eyes shone with a feverish brightness.

"Adolf," I exclaimed, "you are ill."

"No, I'm not ill," he answered impatiently—"I mustn't be ill. But come, come—"

"Where?"

"I'll tell you."

I followed him out into the cold, stormy December morning with a feeling of anxiety that increased every moment.

"Where is the nearest telegraph-office?" he asked.

"A good way off; what are we to do there?"

"Come on—and don't ask so many questions."

Seeing how excited he was, I accompanied him in silence. When we at length reached the door of the telegraph-office, he said:

"And now, please, will you do something for me? Will you telegraph to your mother and ask her if it is true that—Rachel Welt is to be married next week—?"

"What? Did you hear that she was?"

"Never mind just now—I'll tell you all afterward; but now, pray, go at once and send off the telegram. Beg for an immediate answer—immediate, you understand. Have mercy on me, and go!"

His words, and the repressed pain in his voice, had all the more effect on me from their contrast with the habitual coldness and reserve of his manner. I went into the office and sent off the telegram. Somehow or

other it never occurred to me until after I had dis-
patched the message, that my people would think it
strange that I should be so much interested in the fate
of Rachel Welt, and I almost smiled at the thought.
But all desire to smile forsook me when I rejoined
Adolf. His face was now flushed, his eyes were shining, and every now and then he shivered as though
with ague. . . .

"You *are* ill," I once more exclaimed. "Come . . ."
And, seizing him by the arm, I took him to the nearest
café—the snow, meanwhile, had begun to fall thick and
fast.

"It's nothing," he answered. "It's only a slight
feverish attack—I must have had a chill—I have been
wandering all night long in the streets. I know what
you're going to say—it was foolish of me, I am quite
aware of that, my medical studies have taught me how
foolish it was ; but I couldn't help it—I couldn't keep
still. . . . When do you expect an answer to your telegram ? " he added, suddenly and quickly.

"Late in the afternoon—perhaps not till night-
fall."

" Not till then ? "

"Remember that Barnow is a hundred and fifty
miles * from here, that there is a dreadful snow-storm,
and that—what is perhaps more to the purpose—Herr
Michalski, the telegraph officer at home, is generally

* An Austrian mile is equal to 4·714 English miles.

drunk, and is in the habit of keeping back tele-
grams till it suits him to deliver them. But you
may trust me to bring you the answer as soon as it
arrives."

"Thank you," he said. "You can not tell what I
have suffered since I was startled by the sudden intelligence."

"Who told you?" I asked.

"I got to-know by a strange accident," he replied.
"I happened to go into one of the surgical wards of
the infirmary yesterday evening; suddenly I heard
some one call me by my name. I went to the bed from
which the voice had come, and there I found a Jewish
lad lying—it was Salomon Pinkus, brother of Chaim
Pinkus, the cattle-dealer at Barnow. Salomon told me
sadly that he had brought some cattle belonging to his
brother to Vienna, had sold them well, and was preparing to return home, when he slipped on some ice in the
street and broke his arm. 'I didn't want to go to Vienna,' he whined—'I was afraid ; but I had to do it,
as my brother could not leave home just then—he is to
be married to Rachel, daughter of the butcher at Barnow, next week.'—'To whom did you say?' I cried,
catching his sound arm in such a firm grip that he
shrieked out that I wanted to break it too. Well, he
afterward told me that his brother's bride was Rachel
Welt—he was sure that I must know her—I think he
chuckled when he said it—'she had refused to marry

Chaim for a long time, but had suddenly come to her
senses again, and was now quite willing to take
him. . . .'

"He told me a good deal more, and though I answered him, I can't remember what I said. I only
know that I ran away from him in the end, and, rush-
ing out-of-doors, paced the streets all night like a madman, unheeding the storm and the cold. What I felt
I can never describe, nor would you understand if I
were to attempt to do so. . . ."

"Poor fellow !" I answered, compassionately.

"No," he cried, passionately, "you couldn't understand, nor would any one. It was not a mere boyish
affair, you see—such a thing would have been impossible to me. It was the first great passion of my life,
and it will be the last. I have poured out all the love
my nature is capable of feeling at that girl's feet, and if
she has deceived me, I shall go mad or die. Believe
me, I am not exaggerating—I can read my own case as
clearly as if it were physical illness from which I am
suffering : as a proof of this, let me tell you that love
never made me blind ; I always saw the difficulties that
would beset Rachel's path and mine. I know that no
one could well imagine anything more opposite than
our habits of mind and opinions on every subject. She
and I have both to thank orthodox Judaism for this.
But I also know that the barriers between us are not
insuperable. If I have been man enough to make my

own life and open a career for myself, I shall also be man enough to raise my wife to my own level. There is only one thing that could crush me—only one: if Rachel were untrue ! . . ."

"And do you think that possible?" I asked.

"I am unwilling to believe it ; no one yields at once to a belief that would make his life worthless in his eyes for evermore—and so I cling to a last hope. That was why I asked you to telegraph. Although it is very improbable that Salomon should have lied to me, yet it is possible that he may have done so ; . . . still, I confess that I have very little hope, for she used to write to me every week regularly, and I haven't heard from her for the last fortnight. . . ."

"But," I asked, "even supposing that the marriage is really fixed for next week, may you not suspect the girl unjustly? What if she were not faithless after all, but forced into this marriage by her relations, God knows how?"

"Impossible," said Adolf, firmly. "If I could have believed in the possibility of such a thing for a single moment, I should have been on my way to Barnow instead of sitting here. I know the girl far too well to entertain such an idea. Rachel is simple-hearted, clear-minded, and immovable. She could not be forced to do anything against her will. If the worst came to the worst, she would rather have run away from her parents and come to me, than have

given way, even though she'd had to beg her bread
from Barnow to Vienna. I know her. . . ."

Adolf and I talked long together on that gloomy
winter morning. At last I persuaded him to go to
the hospital and do his usual work, promising at the
same time to bring him the telegram, whatever it
might contain, the very moment that it arrived.

It did not come until early on the following
morning, so our worthy fellow - townsman, Herr
Michalski, must have been celebrating some festival on the preceding evening. It ran as follows:
"Yes; Rachel is going to marry Pinkus the cattle-
dealer next Tuesday. But what does it matter to
you?"

Alas! it mattered much more to me at that
moment than my dear mother imagined. I immediately sent for a drosky, and drove to Marien-
gasse, where Adolf had taken a little room. My
heart beat when I pulled the bell.

His old housekeeper came out to meet me.

"Thank God that you've come!" she exclaimed
joyfully as soon as she saw me. "I've been so
dreadfully anxious all night. Just think, another
letter came from Poland yesterday for the Herr
Doctor; I knew where it came from by the stamp;
well, I put it carefully in his flat candlestick that
he might find it the very moment he came home. If
I had only guessed what was in that letter—I'm an

honest woman, sir, and have never stolen anything
in my life, but I should have destroyed it, God forgive me! and thought it a good deed. For, just
listen, sir. He came home early yesterday evening
and asked me breathlessly if you had been here.
'No,' said I—'but there's a letter for you from Poland.' 'Where?' said he, running into his room and
snatching up his letter. There must have been something dreadful in that letter, sir, for the doctor turned
as pale as death, and shivered all over. Then, suddenly, he threw the letter away and began to laugh
aloud—it made my blood run cold to hear him, it
was such a mad laugh. Then he looked about him
like this "—the old woman tried to put on an insane
stare—" and shouted to me to go away—and—God
forgive me!—I was so frightened that I ran away
as quickly as I could. All was silent for a time,
but soon I heard the doctor walking up and down,
up and down, very quickly, and then he threw himself on the sofa and moaned quite low. I can't describe it, it made me shiver with terror; for, you see,
a dreadful thing happened in this very house about
two years ago. My neighbor's lodger, a young
apothecary, poisoned himself because his sweetheart
was false to him. I heard him moan just like the
doctor last night; and I couldn't help thinking that
it was the same story over again. So at last I summoned courage and went into the room. He started

up, and stared at me as if he didn't know who I was.
'It's only me,' I said; 'are you ill?'—'No,' said he,
'I only want to be alone,' so I went away again, but
the whole night long . . ."

I left the old woman talking, and hastened to my
friend's room.

Adolf was sitting motionless in his arm-chair, his
face buried in his hands—it almost seemed as if he
must be asleep, he was so very still. When he
heard the sound of my steps, he let his hands fall to
his side and got up. I never saw the stamp of grief
more strongly·marked on any human face than on
his as he turned toward me.

"Read that," he said, hoarsely, at the same time
pushing a letter nearer me that was lying on the
table. I read as follows:

"HERR DOCTOR : Forgive me for not having
written sooner to tell you that I had made a mistake. I find that I do not love you. I had mistaken friendship for love. I soon found out that
this was the case, but was afraid to write to you
sooner. That is why I only write now, the week
before I am married to Chaim. Perhaps you may
think that I am forced to marry him by my father, but that is not the case—I do it willingly.
Forgive me, Herr Doctor—it was a mistake.

"RACHEL."

"It was a mistake!" cried Adolf in despair, and then sank fainting on the floor.

    .   .   .   .

One spring morning, more than four years after that gloomy winter day when Adolf received the news of Rachel's treachery, I was seated in a large dull house in Vienna bending over a manuscript.

My servant came into the room and gave me a card, saying that the gentleman was waiting to see whether I could receive him.

I looked at the card, and on seeing the name of Dr. Adolf Leiblinger, rushed to the outer door and opened it.

I had not seen my friend for two years. We had never met since the day when he came to me and said very quietly and unconcernedly : "I have accepted a medical appointment under the Dutch Government, and am to start for Batavia immediately. Good-by!"

He was very little changed. His pale face, with its unalterable expression of calm defiance, had only grown browner and darker in the tropical climate where he had lived during the last year or two.

"So you've come back to Europe!" I exclaimed joyfully. "I am so glad. You remember how earnestly I tried to dissuade you from carrying out your project. Going to that murderous climate was neither more nor less than a sort of suicide on your part."

"Yes, it was so," he answered, calmly, "you're quite right."

"You'll remain here now that you've come back, won't you?"

"Yes. My life is not a happy one even now, but it is no longer miserable. I am, and always shall be, indifferent to death; but so long as I live it shall be my endeavor to make my life as useful as possible. I shall settle down either here or in some other university town, as assistant professor."

"I am very glad to hear it," I said. "I never lost hope that time would bring you healing."

"If you call this healing, it was not time that brought it, but—a letter."

"A letter!"

"Yes—from Barnow—from *her*. As soon as I got it I set out for Europe—and went straight to Barnow. I think that I traveled quicker than any one ever did before,—and yet I arrived too late."

"She is dead?" I asked in a low voice.

"Yes; she died four weeks ago."

"She called you to visit her on her deathbed then?"

"As you know the whole story, I will let you read her letter."

He put it in my hand.

It was written in trembling and scarcely legible characters, and ran as follows:

"Spring will soon be here, but I feel that I shall not live to see it, so I will write to you now when I have strength. I do so partly for my own sake, but far more for yours. For my sake, that you may not despise me after I am dead, and for yours, that you may no longer have the pain of feeling that the woman you loved was unworthy of you.

"I lied in that letter which I wrote to you four years ago. I loved you then, love you now, and shall love you till I die. And if God grants that we are the same in heaven as on earth, I shall love you even after death. And it was because I loved you that I parted from you.

"Do not shake your head in despair at these strange words.

"Happiness that I had purchased at the expense of my father's curse and my mother's despair would not have been pure and unsullied. But I should have lived that down.

" *One* thing alone I could not have got over—you smiled at me for saying so long ago, and yet I was right: my ignorance unfitted me for the position your wife would have to hold.

"I had lived too long, in a little provincial town, a gray, still life passed in utter ignorance of the world and its ways; I could not have borne an active life and the full light of day. I should not have been able rightly to understand you either in

sorrow or in joy, and that would have been terrible
to me, and perhaps even more terrible to you. I
should never have been at my ease with your friends
or their wives ; they would have laughed at my
manners and mode of speaking, and I should have
been hurt and you also. You would then perhaps
have kept me shut out from society, and I could
not have borne that. The thought that my husband
was ashamed of me would have been agony to me—
as well as to you. And so the time would have
surely come of which I once warned you : you
would have cursed the hour when I became your
wife. You would not have separated from me—
I know that. But we should have been unhappy,
and you, perhaps, would have been even more unhappy than I.

"I saw all this clearly, and I loved you so dearly
that I did not want you to be made miserable
through me. So I determined that the sorrow should
all be mine—told my parents that I would marry
Chaim, and wrote that letter to you.

"Though I lied to you, I told Chaim the whole
truth. I told him my story, and said that I could
only be his faithful servant and helper. He answered
that time would put all right. I knew that it would
have no effect, but I had taken up my burden and
would bear it.

"It was right, and I do not complain.

"But, alas! I must needs confess that I was too weak to bear my weight of sorrow. I have become pale and ill, and my heart beats so quickly at times that I often faint. I am growing so much weaker that I feel that death must be drawing very near. But I have no fear of death, and I thank God for His goodness in letting me suffer for so short a time, instead of for a long term of years. What good would a long life have been to me?

"Ever since the day I formed the resolution never to be your wife, I have looked forward to writing you one letter that should tell you the whole truth before I died. I never thought that the happiness would have come to me so soon of justifying my conduct in your eyes.

"My life is drawing to a close—our God is truly a merciful God. And now, let me thank you once more for all your love for me. You have been the light and joy of my poor dark life. You made me happy, and are innocent of causing my sorrow. Forgive all the pain that I have brought upon you. It is my last entreaty, and I am dying.

"Ah no!—I have something else to beg of you, and if you do not grant my request, I shall find no rest in the grave.

"Your friend, the doctor's son, told his people in one of his letters that you were now living in a distant land, where the sun is very hot, and where nearly

11

all foreigners die of a malignant fever. He wrote that you had probably gone there because my marriage had caused you misery and despair. I can not tell you what I suffered when I heard that, and were I to attempt to do so you would hardly believe it. But I entreat of you, leave that deadly climate. My heart tells me that you are the greatest and best doctor that ever lived. Come home and help poor sick people.

"Your mother's old prayer-book, that you gave me long ago, shall be buried with me.

"Farewell! May your life be as long and happy as I wish it to be! I shall be dead when you read this letter. RACHEL."

I silently returned the letter to my friend.

He rose, and said as quietly as before: "Now you know why I am going to remain in Europe. Good-by for the present."

But when we had taken each other's hand in silence, the proud reserved man broke down utterly. With a low heart-broken sob, he ejaculated:

"Why couldn't it have been otherwise? Why?..."

I know not what answer to make to this question any more than he did, and so I do not venture to add another word to the story of Rachel Welt, who used to be known in Barnow by the name of "Esterka Regina."

"BARON SCHMULE."

(1874.)

"BARON SCHMULE."

WHEN driving from Barnow toward the south, to
Bukowina or Moldavia, a grand castle may be seen
perched on the top of a hill at about three hours'*
distance from Barnow. It is situated near Z——, at
which place the highroad crosses the Dniester, and
it stands so high that its white walls and shimmer-
ing windows may be seen from a great distance.
It is surrounded by beautiful pleasure-grounds, which
extend over the hill, and stretch far out into the
plain below. It is, perhaps, the most beautiful place
in Podolia, and is certainly better kept up than any
other. Its owner is known far and wide as "Baron
Schmule;" for although he is now the powerful
Freiherr Sigismund von Ronnicki, he began life as
Schmule Runnstein.

His success was rapid and wonderful, for he went
straight as an arrow toward his object, without wast-
ing time by looking to the right hand or to the left.

* About fifteen English miles.

Very few people can do that. Most men resemble
tops, for they are quite satisfied with making rapid
and noisy gyrations, and do not perceive that they
never leave the spot from which they started, but
are only turning round and round upon their own
axis; while the arrow, which Baron Schmule resembled, neither hastens nor lags in its flight, but makes
straight for the mark. Putting metaphor aside, let
me say that Baron Schmule knew what he wanted,
and attained the object for which he strove as
quickly and certainly as if he had had two eyes to
guide him on his way instead of one.

Like every one else, he began life as a top; but
something happened that changed his whole character, and with his character, his career. That something was a *blow with a riding-whip*. It is a strange
story. . . .

More than fifty years ago a poor widow lived in
Z—— with her son. She strove to make enough to
feed and clothe them both by the proceeds of her
trade of confectioner—a poor one to follow in a
place so small as Z——. She was called Miriam
Runnstein. The little boy began to help his mother
as soon as he could walk and count: he had to sell
the sweetmeats that his mother made, and used to per-
ambulate the streets, calling, "Who'll buy 'Fladen'?
'Fladen' and almond comfits! who'll buy? who'll
buy?"

But very few people in the Ghetto make a practice of eating sweetmeats, and a marriage or circumcision feast, on which occasion a confectioner is hired for the day, is not of constant occurrence. Pennies came in very slowly, and poor little Schmule often cried with hunger, as he walked about trying to sell the sugar-plums in his basket.

His best customers lived at the castle, about half a mile * from the town. This castle belonged to Baron Wodnicki. Alfred Wodnicki was a very rich man—so rich that, although he was a great spendthrift, he could not manage to squander much more than the income accruing from his immense property. He lived very little at the castle, for he was soon bored by the quietness and dullness of country life, so he spent most of his time at Paris or Baden-Baden. He always went to Baden-Baden when his wife was in Paris, and to Paris when she was at Baden-Baden. The husband and wife got on very well together now that they had agreed to live separate lives. Their only child, young Baron Wladislaus, did not live at the castle either, but had been sent to a celebrated Jesuit seminary at Krakau.

So the servants had the castle all to themselves. There is an old Polish proverb that runs very much to this effect : "Who is so idle and has so sweet a tooth as a lackey !" The proverb was true in this

* A little more than two English miles.

case at least. Little Schmule always found purchasers for his wares when he had succeeded in dragging his heavy basket up the hill, and so he used often to go there both in summer and winter, although it was a long way for such a little fellow to walk with his burden. It is true that he got as many boxes on the ear as pence, but what did he care for that?—a Jewish child was used to such treatment!

So time went on, till Schmule was thirteen years old. Who knows how long he might have gone on hawking his mother's "Fladen" and almond comfits about the country-side, if something had not happened that changed the whole course of his life.

One very hot day in August Schmule set out for the castle. The sun was blazing down upon him, and the great heat made him pant as he toiled up the steep ascent leading to the castle; but he almost ran, he was so eager to get to the top—and no wonder. It was between eleven and twelve on a Friday morning, and there was not a penny at home with which to buy the Sabbath dinner. If hunger is hard to bear on an ordinary day, it is much worse on the Sabbath, when there is more time to think of it.

As Schmule hastened along, he was far too busy thinking of what had to be bought on his return to Z——, to look about him, or to keep his ears open; and so he never heard a horse galloping up the drive, until it was so close to him that he only saved him-

self from being ridden over by a hasty spring on one
side.

The rider was a pale-faced youth, with a fowling-
piece at his side, and turned out to be young Baron
Wladislaus Wodnicki, who had come home to spend
his summer holidays. He laughed heartily when he
saw what a fright he had given the Jewish boy, who
was still trembling too much to remember to touch his
cap. He then turned his horse and rode slowly up to
Schmule, till he almost touched him. The latter meanwhile pressed as close as he could to the wall of rock
that bordered the drive.

"Why didn't you touch your cap to me, you
rascal?" asked the young Baron, raising his riding-
whip.

"Because — I — was — so — frightened," stammered
Schmule.

The young man lowered his riding-whip, and after
a few moments' thought, burst into a loud laugh.

"You're afraid of the horse, are you?" he asked;
"very well, then, go and stand there," pointing to the
middle of the road. "Don't you hear me? *There!*"
he repeated, angrily; and the boy obeyed with mani-
fest terror. "Now, then," he continued, "don't move
from there till I allow you—do you understand? It'll
be the worse for you if you move," and snatching up
his gun, he went on. "I swear, by all the saints, that
I'll shoot you down like a mad dog if you move!"

After saying this he rode on, and then turned again, and galloped down the drive straight at the boy.

Schmule watched the horse approaching him with the fascination of terror—a mist came over his eyes—in another moment he jumped out of the way and—the horse, instead of hitting him, only knocked the basket of sweetmeats from his back, scattering its contents all over the dusty road. The boy also fell, but only from nervous fear.

"You did move, you scoundrel!" cried Baron Wladislaus, putting his gun to his shoulder. Suddenly he changed his mind, and restoring his fowling-piece to its place, rushed at the boy with his riding-whip. The latter, in order to avoid as much as possible the violent blows that were aimed at him, now with the end and now with the knob of the whip, threw himself at the young man's feet.

All at once Schmule uttered a heart-rending shriek, and fell senseless on the ground.

And then Baron Wladislaus rode away.

An hour later a kind-hearted peasant took the unconscious boy in his hay-cart to the little Jewish town, and gave him to his mother. It is unnecessary to say what the poor woman felt when she saw her boy's disfigured countenance and senseless state—such things are better not described.

The doctor came, restored Schmule to consciousness, and washed and bound up his wounds. He said

that the boy would soon be quite well again, but that
the sight of his right eye was gone for ever.

Schmule had an unexpected visitor on the first day
that he was able to get out of bed. Fat Gregor, the
young Baron's valet, came to see him. He brought
the boy two ducats, and told him that his master was
ready and willing to pay both the doctor and apothecary, if he would forbear making any complaint to
the magistrate of his conduct.

"Go!" cried Schmule—that was all that he said
—but his remaining eye glared so savagely at Gregor,
that the latter thought discretion the better part of
valor, and beat a hasty retreat. As soon as he got
back to the castle, he went to his master, and said:
"Beg your pardon, Herr Baron, you've sent the Jew
stark-staring mad as well as knocked out his eye—he
was more like a wild beast than anything else."

When Schmule was able to go out again, his first
walk was to the court of justice. The leader of the
synagogue offered to go with him, but he said he
wanted to go alone. "Thank you," he said; "but it
isn't necessary. I am no longer a child—that blow
has made me ten years older. Besides that, I only
want justice."

He went to the judge and made his complaint.
The trial began, and was carried on as—well as all
such trials were in those days. What chance had a
poor Jewish boy against a Polish noble long ago?

None! But the trial had one merit: it was short. The persons interested in it were not long kept in suspense as to what the verdict was to be. All was settled in the space of a month. Schmule was then cited to appear before the court, and the Herr Mandatar said to him very sternly: "Your story was a lie, Jew! You did not get out of the Herr Baron's way, but insisted on pressing close up to the horse, and so you were accidentally struck by the riding-whip. You may be thankful that Baron Wladislaus has been good enough to pardon you for making such a calumnious charge against him, otherwise you might have been tried for perjury! Now—go!"

Schmule went home.

When he entered his mother's kitchen, the good woman was so startled by the look on his face, that she exclaimed, in terror: "Child, child! what is the matter? Has anything worse happened?"

"Yes," he answered, "something much worse—justice has been denied me." His voice here died away into an indistinct murmur, but at last his mother heard him say: "I will do as the Herr Mandatar advised me—I will be grateful for Baron Wladislaus's kindness. . . ."

"Son!" cried the old woman, in a voice of agony. "I know what you're going to do. I can read it in your face. You're going to steal into the castle and murder him in his sleep! . . ."

"No," replied Schmule, with a smile. "That wouldn't do at all, for they would hang me for murder, and who would take care of you then? No, my vengeance must be of another kind—I must become a rich man."

"God has darkened your understanding, my son," moaned the old woman. But she wept still more bitterly when Schmule told her that he had made up his mind to go to Barnow. He sold the only things that belonged to him, which would not be required now that he was going away—his bed and bedding. The sale of these articles brought him five gulden in all, because at the last moment he threw in some prayer-books that he did not want. As he was going away he promised to send his mother a share of his earnings.

He went to Barnow with his little store of five gulden, or about five florins in English money, in his pocket, and there set up a little pack, consisting of matches, soap, pomade, and feathers. He sold his merchandise at the inns and in the streets. And, as he was untiring in his labors, and spent very little on himself, he was able both to support his mother and to lay by a little money.

In two years' time he was so far beforehand with the world, that he gave up this mode of gaining his livelihood, and bought a large store of goods such as country people require. He then began to travel about the country-side as a peddler; and a very hard life he led. Like Nathan Bilkes, the father of Frau Christine, he wandered about, with a great pack on his back, from village to village, and from fair to fair. He was seldom paid in money for his goods, but received fruit and skins instead. This circumstance, however, was of advantage to him.

After having worked as a peddler for three years, he returned to Barnow, and set up a stall for small-wares in a corner of the market-place. His success was so great that he was soon able to rent a real shop, and to keep his mother more comfortably. But he remained as abstemious as before with regard to himself. His food consisted for the most part of dry bread, for he only allowed himself the luxury of a bit of meat upon the Sabbath.

His mother died when he was twenty-three—that is, ten years after he left Z——. She died in his arms. When he had buried her, and the eight days of mourning were over, he went to Czernowitz, which is a larger town than Barnow. As chance would have it, Baron Wladislaus Wodnicki, who had just taken the management of his estates into his own hands, drove past him in his phaeton, as he was leaving the little town of Z——. "I am glad to have seen him," said Schmule to his traveling companion; "for otherwise grief might have made me idle for some time to come."

Schmule was now alone in the world, but still he

worked as hard as if he had had a large family to support, and so he gradually became well to do in the world. He was much respected as an honorable man, fair in all his dealings; and this, added to his wealth, enabled him to gain the hand in marriage of one of the richest heiresses in Czernowitz, in spite of his having only one eye. After his marriage he increased his business considerably, and became well known in the commercial world as Samuel Runnstein, the dry-salter. And again, as if this did not give him enough to do, he set up a large wine business, in addition to the other.

Schmule now showed for the first time to their full extent the marvelous powers of work and determination of character that he possessed. He traveled all over Germany and France, Russia and Moldavia, setting up agencies everywhere. Ten years later he was looked upon as the richest merchant in the whole district.

At length his wife died, leaving him a little daughter. Schmule now sold the good-will of both the wine and dry-salting businesses, and became a corn-merchant. He bought in Podolia, Bessarabia, and Moldavia, and sold in the Western markets. There was only one landowner from whom he would buy nothing, and that was Baron Wladislaus Wodnicki: although the bailiff offered him very good bargains, he was not to be tempted. The unfortu-

nate bailiff had rather a hard time of it—he found
it so difficult to provide his master with a large and
constant supply of money. For Wladislaus succeeded
in doing what the old Baron had never done : every
month he spent as much as his estates brought in
in the year. His wife, a French lady, did her part
in squandering her husband's wealth. And so the
bailiff came to Schmule and begged him to buy some
corn, but he refused, saying with a strange smile : "I
made a vow more than five - and - twenty years ago
that I would only do *one* stroke of business with your
master ; and the time for that has not come yet. . . ."

Years passed, and Schmule grew richer and richer.
He married again, and his wife brought him a large
fortune.   Then came the year 1848, with its revo-
lutionary restlessness ; and Schmule, who knew how
to turn everything to his advantage, became a millionaire.   He was now known as Herr Sigismund
Runnstein, and the Russian Government employed
him to provision their army in Hungary. By this
means he made a great deal more money.   After
that he gave up business, and when any one wanted
him to undertake some new project, he refused, alleg-
ing that he preferred to wait.

He had not long to wait. It is quite possible to
squander even a colossal fortune if one has a mind
to do it. Two years later, Baron Wladislaus and his
wife were obliged to leave Paris. They returned to

Z——, but even there they found it difficult to get enough money to live on; for their estates were so deeply mortgaged that not a blade of grass could really be said to belong to them, and their creditors became more and more troublesome every day. After a time, the Baroness went back to her own people in France, and the Baron, who had to remain at Z—— whether he would or not, sought comfort first in champagne, and afterward, when that became too expensive a luxury, in schnapps.

At length one day he found himself no longer beset by his creditors. Schmule had bought up all the claims against him, although they amounted to many thousand pounds sterling. "It's the first bad bargain that Schmule Runnstein ever made," said all his friends. But the general astonishment was much increased when it was discovered that he apparently let things alone after that, and took no steps to foreclose.

But in spite of appearances, he had not been idle. He sent a petition to the Emperor, begging for leave to buy an estate; for in those days the Galician Jews were legally incapacitated from holding land. He even went to Vienna, to support his cause in person. But all in vain. "If I had committed murder," said Schmule when he came home, "I might perhaps have persuaded the Government to let me off; but this request they will not grant."

He wandered about for many days, lost in deep and melancholy thought. At last, after a terrible struggle, he determined on the course he meant to pursue. He went to his wife, whom he loved dearly, and said to her : "I have made up my mind to be baptized and become a Christian. Don't look so frightened, and don't cry—listen to me quietly. I *must* do it. My whole life would otherwise be a lie, a folly, a failure. I must become possessor of the Wodnicki estates. I have lived poorly and worked hard—harder perhaps than any other man on the face of the earth. And now it is not a reward that I demand, but my just right. This is the *only* way that I can attain it, so it must be done. But you shall choose for yourself ; I leave you free. How dearly I love you I need not say, but still I repeat—I will not oppose your decision, whatever it may be. . . ."

She loved him too, but she could not give up her religion, and so they parted.

Schmule became a member of the Roman Catholic Church, and took the name of Sigismund Ronnicki. His daughter by his first marriage, who was nearly grown up, was baptized at the same time, and received the name of Maria.

The conversion of the rich Jew and his daughter was the theme of endless conversation in the neighborhood.

The day after he had been received into the Christian Church, Schmule foreclosed all the mortgages he held upon Wladislaus's estates, and, as was to be expected, the land went at a very low price. Schmule bought it. The Baron disappeared — no one knew where he had gone ; and Schmule took up his abode at the castle of Z——, with his daughter Maria.

In the year 1854, when the army was so much increased that the state was greatly in want of money, Schmule bought himself the title of "Freiherr" for a large sum.

But still he used to say, "I haven't got all that I want yet—my full right."

But the time was fast approaching when this strange man's last wish was to be fulfilled.

One day an announcement was made in the Polish newspapers, to the effect that a comfortable home and suitable maintenance had been provided for that irredeemable vagabond and drunkard, Baron Wladislaus Wodnicki, by the kindness of a noble-minded benefactor.

And so it was. The "noble-minded benefactor" was Baron Sigismund Ronnicki, who had literally picked the "vagabond" out of the streets of Barnow, where he was wandering houseless and forlorn, and had taken him home to his castle at Z——. Wladislaus was given everything he wanted except—schnapps. And why was this, and this alone, denied him? "When he drinks schnapps," said Schmule, "he forgets everything that has happened. And I intend that he should remember. I will have my right."

But the "drunkard" was not to be long a source of satisfaction to the new lord of the castle. At midsummer, in the year following, a great feast was given by Schmule, in honor of his daughter's marriage to a Magyar noble. During the evening Wodnicki succeeded in getting some schnapps. He drank freely, and then staggered out of doors, and down the drive in which he had met the Jewish boy fifty years before.

He never returned to the castle.

Next morning he was found lying dead under the steep wall of rock that bounded one side of the drive. Whether he had fallen over the precipice in his drunken blindness, or had thrown himself over, no one ever knew.

This is one of the many strange stories that take place on this earth of ours.

THE PICTURE OF CHRIST.

(1868.)

THE PICTURE OF CHRIST.

. . . . How distinctly I can see the little town even
now, with its narrow, tortuous, and gloomy streets, its
ruined castle on the top of the hill, and its stately
monastery near the river! It is to this last that I
wish to draw the reader's attention. The Dominican
monastery is a huge pile of buildings surrounded by
a wall in which one can still see the traces of the old
Tartar attacks of long ago. Within the wall is a
confused mass of chapels and dwelling-houses, separated from each other by damp, moss-grown courtyards, or by sparsely covered grass-plots. I often
went there in my boyhood, and used to like playing
among the graves in the little churchyard. I also delighted in listening to the echo of my footsteps in
the great empty refectory; but I liked best of all to
go to the "Abbot's Chapel," a small Byzantine building which was known by that name, and look up
at a picture that had been hung there a short time
before. It had been painted by the proud and

beautiful Gräfin Jadwiga Bortynska, lady of the manor of Barnow. It was a wonderful picture—breathing love and peace. Christ was represented standing on vaporous clouds, His hands stretched out in blessing over the earth. The pale face, which was, as it were, framed in black curls, had an expression of divine love and sublime goodness—perfect man and perfect God.

But I did not think of that when I first saw the picture, for I was then only a thoughtless boy of twelve years old. It was on a bright, warm autumn day that I saw it first. An hour after it was hung up in its place, little Wladik, the sexton's son, showed it to me. The sunshine was falling full upon it at the time, and I almost started as I saw the life-like figure in its dark frame.

"Do you know who it is?" I asked my school-fellow.

"How can you ask?" he exclaimed with boyish indignation. "It is our Lord Jesus Christ, whom the Jews crucified."

"No, Wladik," I answered with the utmost decision, "it isn't; it's Bocher David, who used to teach me until last spring."

Wladik was very angry, and scolded me well for saying such a dreadful thing, but he could not convince me that I was wrong: I knew what I knew. When I went home in the evening I told my father about the picture.

"Silly child," he said with a smile; "who could have painted it?"

"Our Frau Gräfin," I replied.

My father looked grave. "Well, well," he said thoughtfully, "it is almost incredible. . . ."

"What?" I asked quickly. But he told me to be quiet.

I should not then have understood what he meant; but I heard the story afterward when I was older—the sad story of that picture of Christ in the chapel at Barnow—and learned that it was also, as I had supposed, a portrait of my old teacher, Bocher David.

It is a strange story, reader, and will seem all the more extraordinary to you, if you have been brought up in a Western home, and have been accustomed from your infancy to civilization and tolerance of others. It is also sad, very sad. But do not blame me for that, for my heart bleeds when I remember this over-true tale, which must be regarded as one of the dark riddles of life, and as the doing of that eternal, inscrutable Power that deals out darkness or light, happiness or misery, to the weak human heart. . . .

I will now tell you the story.

.   .   .   .

The small town of Barnow lies in the middle of an immense plain. Close to it is the only hill for several miles around, and on the top of this little hill are the ruins of a castle where the lords of Barnow, or Barecki Starosts, used to live. The last of this race, an old man, weak in mind as in body, now lives in his cheerless house by the river-side; while the new lord of the manor, Graf Bortynski, lives in a new and splendid castle in the plain, far away from the one-storied cottages, the rickety little houses, the narrow, airless streets of Barnow, and all the want and misery of the people who inhabit them.

But these inhabitants of Barnow are happy, their streets are light and airy, and their houses comfortable, in comparison with those who have to live in that part of the town which is built in the unhealthy marshes near the river. It is always dark and gloomy there, however brightly the sun may shine, and dark pestiferous vapors fill the air, although the meadows beyond may be full of flowers. And this wretched part of the town is the most thickly inhabited of all, for it is the Ghetto, the Jews' quarter, or, as they call it in Barnow, the "Gasse."

David was the strangest and most mysterious-looking figure in the "Gasse," which was anyhow only too full of such people—for when plants are kept in the dark they are apt to take eccentric forms. He was the son of the former rabbi of the town. Even in his boyhood he had been the pride and

delight of his father, and indeed of the whole community. His bright young intelligence was early
able to comprehend the secrets of the Talmud, its
subtleties and riddles, and the boy was looked upon
with wondering admiration by all. For, pale and
delicate as he was, the Jews of Barnow believed that
he would live to become a great scribe, learned in
the Scriptures. So they forgave his hastiness and
fits of passion.

In course of time the old rabbi died, and left his
widow and only child nothing but his great library
and the love of the whole congregation. The community did what they could for the widow and
orphan, or rather did what they thought proper and
necessary. David and his mother were allowed to
remain in the small back rooms of their old house,
and the front rooms were given to the new rabbi.
It was right and fitting that it should be so, but it
wounded the child's feelings. David no longer heard
the words of praise that he had been accustomed to,
although he deserved them more and more every day;
so he became ever more defiant, and was conse-
quently very much disliked. It happened one day
that he excelled the rabbi in his interpretation of a
passage of the Talmud, and afterward told different
people that he had done so, and thus made an enemy
in the community. He was now as much disliked
as he had once been praised. His position grew

unbearable. But as long as his mother lived, he remained at Barnow. She was the only person he obeyed, and she alone could sometimes bring a smile to the grave, sad face of her son. One morning soon after her death, which happened when he was fifteen, David disappeared. No one knew what had become of him. He was soon forgotten, and was only spoken of now and then as the late rabbi's son, a wise and learned youth, but wicked and wrong-headed to an extraordinary degree.

He remained away for twelve long years.

At length he returned unexpectedly, and rented one of the small rickety houses in the little Podolian town. On the following day he went to the elders of the synagogue, and to those men who were appointed to nurse the sick, and told them that he had determined to devote his life to the care of the sick and dying. He said that he knew many simples, and a good deal about the art of healing, and entreated them to grant his request, and not to spare him when .he could be of any use. They were astonished at his resolution, and praised him for his goodness. But as time went on they learned really to appreciate his help, and blessed him ; then once more his praises were repeated from mouth to mouth as of yore. But there was a certain air of mystery about him, for he made no intimacies in the "Gasse." No one knew what studies he was engaged in when his

night-lamp burned till early morning ; no one knew
what were his resources, or where he had been during
his absence from Barnow. The rabbi, who had long
forgotten David's boyish faults, and my father — because he was the town doctor—used to see a good
deal of him, and they were the only people with
whom he was on familiar terms. It was discovered
through them that he had been in the Holy Land,
that he had seen the countries of the West, and that
he had even crossed the great ocean, and had spent
some time in "Amerikum," as it was called in the
language of the "Gasse." It was said that he could
speak many foreign tongues, that he knew everything,
and could do whatever he chose, whether good or
evil, for he was a master of the "Cabala," and well
acquainted with the great and terrible secrets of the
"Sohar," the Cabalist primer ; and, finally, that he had
sworn to himself that he would never marry, and so
he was still a "bocher," or bachelor.

But he either knew nothing of these rumors, or
did not care what people said of him. He helped all
who were in need of his assistance, without desiring
either thanks or payment. And as time passed on, all
began to feel a deep respect, and even love, for the
pale silent man who did so much for them. His face
had quite lost the gloomy passionate expression of his
boyhood, and had become at once grave and gentle.
While every one felt a fearless confidence in his kind-

ness and sympathy, no one would have ventured to treat him with familiarity. The "Bocher" was the only inhabitant of the Ghetto whom the Christian boys neither pelted nor scorned, although outwardly he was only distinguished from his brethren in the faith by the careful cleanliness of his clothing. He wore the same curious old-fashioned Polish garments as all the other Jews in Poland and Russia; and no dress could have shown off to better advantage his tall stately figure, and pale intellectual face surrounded by clustering curls of black hair.

This man was my teacher from my sixth till my twelfth year. I was a very mischievous boy, always ready for fun, and hating to sit still, and he treated me with continual grave kindness. We seldom exchanged a word that had not to do with the lessons he was teaching me. But once it was different: it was on the day on which I had gone to the monastery school for the first time. I came home weeping bitterly because of the contemptuous way in which my school-fellows had treated me for my religion's sake. The "Bocher" came in, and I told him of my distress. He listened to me in silence, and then opened the Bible at the place where he had given me my last lesson on the previous evening. My tears would not stop. "Don't cry," he said; "don't cry, my child, 'they know not what they do.'" And then he added, in a harsh stern tone, such as I had never heard from him before : "Don't cry. They are not worth your tears. And a day of retribution will come sooner or later." I looked up at him in surprise, and saw that his face wore a strange threatening expression. He was silent for a time, and gradually the fierce look faded away. Then he explained the passage to me in a quiet voice. . . . .

I was his only pupil during all these years, but all at once he gave up teaching me. A strange and important event had taken place in his own life, which made him wish me to leave him. I only spoke to him once afterward.

  .   .   .   .

Old Graf Adam Bortynski was a hard man, loved by none and feared by all. He belonged to a younger branch of the Bortynskis, and so had had very little chance of ever becoming head of the family. He seldom lived in the country, and had his rents sent to him in Paris, London, Monaco, or Homburg. Very little was known about him in Barnow, when he suddenly came there as master at the death of young Graf Arthur, who died in Paris of apoplexy brought on by intemperance. People used to whisper mysteriously in Barnow about that time that no one had had such an evil influence on the late lord of the manor as his present successor, Graf Adam.

But, however that might be, Graf Adam was mas-

ter now. He had never married, although he was by
no means a woman-hater; but on becoming head of
the family, he made up his mind that it was his
duty to do so. He chose lovely Jadwiga Polanska
to be his wife. She was the daughter of an im-
poverished noble in the vicinity. Every one knew
that she feared and hated Graf Bortynski, but it
was also known that her father had sold her to
him; and several people who were better informed
than the rest could have told the price that had
been paid for her to a farthing. For years afterward the inhabitants of the little town used to
talk about the wedding procession, and tell how
proud and triumphant Graf Adam had looked that
day, and how his bride had walked beside him pale
as death, and with an expression of deep wretched-
ness. The breakfast was very grand, and went off
well; but at an early hour on the following morning, the servants heard a shot fired in the wing in
which the rooms of the newly-married couple were,
and on hastening there they found Graf Adam in
his room, shot through the head, the pistol still
convulsively clutched in his right hand. No one
knew what had induced him to commit suicide in
this unexpected way, and the pale young widow
never said a word to clear up the mystery.

The story formed the subject of endless discussion and conjecture, until something else happened

to take its place. Such things are not of uncommon occurrence in Poland and Russia! The estates went to the heir of entail, the head of a distant branch of the family, and Gräfin Jadwiga inherited the castle and town of Barnow.

It seemed fated that the castle should remain uninhabited, for even the young widow went away. She was eighteen when she left Barnow, and it was years before she returned. Rumors were current of her triumphs as a beauty and a wit in Paris, Heligoland, or Baden-Baden. She did not marry again, as every one expected. One spring day she returned to Barnow, after an absence of nearly ten years. The castle was once more inhabited, and its courtyards were full of life and bustle. Gräfin Jadwiga had grown rather stouter than of old, but she was still beautiful, marvelously beautiful, in spite of what some people would have thought the too great pallor of her face.

.   .   .   .

One fine morning in May two young people were out riding together, and enjoying the freshness and brightness of the weather.

Were they happy? The rapid movement and the fresh morning air had brought a tinge of color to the lady's pale face which was very becoming to her. The Gräfin Jadwiga looked bright and sweet that day, and really happy. Her companion did not

look either so cheerful or so happy as she did. He
was a young man with fair hair, the stature of a
giant, and the heart of a child. Scandal-mongers
even went so far as to say that he was like a child
in intellect also. But however that may be, it is
true that Baron Starsky loved Gräfin Jadwiga with
all the intensity of *first* love, as he used to call it,
when he forgot that he had once talked "love" to
his mother's pretty little French maid. But that
was long ago—fully six months ago. He was very
rich, his estates adjoined those of the Gräfin, but he
would have loved her even had this not been the
case. He wanted to have told her all this during
that morning's ride, and to have asked her to be his
wife; but he had had no opportunity. Who could
make an offer to a woman when riding at a hand-
gallop?

At length Gräfin Jadwiga grew tired of what
Baron Starsky inwardly called the "mad pace" at
which she had been going. The horses panted as
they returned toward the town at a walk; but,
strangely enough, the palpitation which Starsky had
before ascribed to the quickness of the pace at which
he had been riding, did not in the least diminish.
It grew worse. The moment for speaking had come,
and he hesitated whether or not to seize it.

He began to talk about the weather, like the good,
stupid, loving giant that he was. He expatiated on

the beauty of the spring, and although as a general rule he cared little or nothing for flowers, he now told Gräfin Jadwiga a great many wonderful things about them. The pauses in their conversation grew longer and longer. At last he saw with terror that he could not keep up this kind of small-talk much longer.

It was as though he had been suddenly relieved of a burden too heavy to be borne, when the Gräfin suddenly reined in her horse, and asked, "What can that curious dark figure down there in the meadow be?"

Baron Starsky put up his eye-glass in order to see better.

"It's a Jew, Gräfin," he said. "But look! he has got something shining in his hand—a zinc box of some kind. What the deuce is he doing with it?"

"Let us ask him."

So saying, the Gräfin leaped the ditch into the meadow, and Starsky of course followed her. The Jew started as though he would have run away, but changing his mind, he waited quietly until the riders approached him. His whole manner showed how timid he was and how little at his ease.

"What are you doing there?" asked Gräfin Jadwiga.

"I am collecting medicinal herbs for my sick people," he replied in pure German.

"You're a doctor!" she inquired in surprise. "That's a strange calling for a tradesman or a Talmudist—and you Jews are all either the one or the other—to pursue in addition to your other work. . . ."

Here Starsky interrupted her by asking somewhat roughly—

"If you're only gathering herbs, why can't you look people full in the face? Why do you breathe so hard—eh, Jew?"

And stooping from the saddle, he seized him firmly by the shoulder. The man wrenched himself free, and in so doing his hat fell off, letting them see his noble, thoughtful face.

"Leave me alone!" he cried, threateningly.

Gräfin Jadwiga hastily thrust her horse between the angry men. She was deadly pale, her breath came quick and fast, and her colorless lips trembled as if she were trying in vain to speak. Her eyes never left the Jew's face.

He meanwhile had recovered his self-possession, and although pale, looked calm and collected.

"Who are you? . . . Is it *really* you? . . . Who are you?" she exclaimed, now in a voice sharpened by anxiety, and again as though in joy. . . .

"My name is David Blum," he answered, in a low toneless voice. "People call me Bocher David. I am a Jewish teacher and sick-nurse in your town. . . ."

She reeled in her saddle and hid her face in her hands.

"My God!" she moaned, "is it a bad dream? . . . It is you, Friedrich! . . . Your voice! . . . Your face! . . Why are you here, and in that dress? . . . Can I be going mad? . . . Friedrich, it *must* be you . . . Friedrich Reimann! . . ."

She dismounted, and going to him, took his hands in hers. Starsky felt his head going round as he watched the scene.

Bocher David had a hard struggle. He turned to go away; then he tried to speak, but could not. At length he managed to force out the words in a low, strained voice: "Friedrich Reimann is dead—has been dead for years. I am David Blum, the sick-nurse."

She drew a long breath.

"I understand you," she said; "Friedrich is dead, but David Blum is alive. And I must say to him what I can no longer say to Friedrich. . . . I have sought you long, long and earnestly. I have found you at last. You must not go until you have listened to me. . . ."

"It would be useless, Frau Gräfin," he answered, gently but firmly. "Friedrich forgave you long ago —forgave you with all his heart. . . ." There was a look of pain on his face as he spoke.

"But it isn't useless," she exclaimed, " or at least

not to me. I entreat you to listen to me only once
—for one hour. Come and see me this afternoon at
the castle. . . ."

He shook his head with a sad smile.

"Don't say no," she continued. "You are a Jew,
and it was a Jew who said, 'Be merciful to the
weak!' It is for mercy that I beg. . . . Oh, come!
. . . For God's sake come, and for the sake of old
times! . . ."

"I promise," he said, after a short pause. Then
silently raising his hat he went away.

Gräfin Jadwiga drew a long breath of relief, passed
her hand across her eyes as if she were waking from
a dream, and then turned to Starksy, who was approaching her with an expression of unmitigated astonishment. They remounted their horses, and returned to Barnow Castle in silence. On getting there
they parted without a word.

Starsky rode home to his father's house in deep
thought, a very unusual circumstance with him. Gräfin
Jadwiga Bortynska and Bocher David . . . His brain
reeled. . . . And this was the woman he would have
asked to be his wife! If he had done so, she would
perhaps have accepted him—*perhaps?*—undoubtedly
—certainly! It was horrible! . . .

The domestic annals of the house of Starsky contained an unwonted occurrence on that day: a youthful member of that noble family ate very little din-

ner, and remained lost in thought during the whole
of the rest of the afternoon! . . .

.   .   .   .

The park at Barnow Castle was very prettily laid
out in flower-beds, and beyond these it was dotted
with clumps of fine old trees. The air was full of
the song of birds and the perfume of spring flowers.
The sun was shining brightly.

A small summer-house was situated in a quiet
corner, and from its windows one could look down
over blossoming elder-bushes upon the blue waters
of the lake, in which the willows at the edge were
mirrored. It was a place to sit and dream in.

But the woman who was seated in the large easy-
chair near the window was not thinking pleasant
thoughts. Her eyes, which were gazing fixedly at
some point in the horizon, saw nothing of the quiet
beauty of the spring landscape. Her expression was
as sad and despairing as her heart. The mask she
wore in public had fallen from her face, and she
looked what she was—an unhappy, sorely tried woman,
and haunted by the bitter memories of the past. . . .

Memories of the past!

The days of childhood and early youth, which
other people look back upon as an Eden of light
and joy, were a time of which she never thought
without a shuddering horror :—the dissipation and
penury of the life in her father's house—a life of

misery and constant dread. . . . Her mother, a pale, broken-hearted woman, who, foreseeing her husband's ruin, had yet been powerless to prevent it, and who had at last faded and died under the weight of a burden too heavy for her to bear. . . . She had been the good angel of the house. After her death matters had come to a climax, and everything had to be sold except a small estate to which Jadwiga and her father had been removed. . . . How distinctly she remembered the following years, with their ever-increasing poverty and shame! This last was the worst—it had been harder to bear than even cold and hunger. And the hopelessness of it all! . . . Her father, indeed, had been able to find continual comfort in all the ills of life in the brandy-bottle, and when he had drunk himself into a good humor and hopefulness, it had irritated him to see his daughter's sad tearful face. On such occasions he used to beat her cruelly in order to make her look cheerful! . . .

As Jadwiga thought of these things her face wore an expression of utter contempt. Alas for those who can only remember their parents with scorn!

She grew up to be a beautiful woman, in spite of her tears and the blows she had to bear. But she cursed her beauty, and she cursed the day on which Graf Adam had first seen her and fallen in love with her. She shuddered as she thought of the day when

he had bought her from her father for ten thousand
Polish gulden; when her father had come to her and
had told her that she must be Gräfin Bortynska, if
she did not wish to see him, a gray-haired old man,
begging his bread from door to door. She remembered how she had thrown herself at his feet, and
entreated him with tears not to give her into the
power of that harsh, cruel old man, whom she hated
and feared, and who, people said, was a murderer.
How she had promised to work for her father and
herself, were it even as a domestic servant, swearing
that he should never, never starve. But all in vain!
. . . A Polanska should never become a household
drudge. . . . And after that she had become Graf
Adam's bride. . . .

Her memory of that time was so vivid that it was
almost more than she could bear. She started up
from her seat, and paced up and down the summer-
house with folded arms and tightly compressed lips.
But it was of no use; one picture of the past after
another rose up before her.

Once more she lived through that time of misery.
She thought of the day when they had dragged her
to church, an unwilling victim, and had forced her to
perjure her soul in the sight of her God; her God,
who had hitherto been the only light and comfort in
her dark life, and whom they had thus, as it were,
made a lie to her. She thought of the marriage-feast,

during which she had first made up her mind that
either she or her husband should die before morning.

She remembered how slowly the minutes had
passed, till she could at length get up and leave the
table. She had gone at once to her room, and finding
her maid waiting for her, had sent her to bed. She had
then turned with loathing from the sight of the luxury
surrounding her, and had busied herself with thoughts
of vengeance on the man who had forced her to marry
him, knowing all the time how she hated him.

Even now, so many years afterward, she could
not help shuddering, when she remembered that she
had suddenly gained sufficient calmness to carry out
the diabolical plan she had thought of. She recol-
lected how she had taken one of the heavy silver
candlesticks on her table, and had gone through all
the echoing passages and rooms in the wing in which
her rooms were situated. She had avoided looking
in any of the mirrors that she passed, fearing to see
her own face, for she had a horror of herself.

She had at last come to the large folding-doors
opening into the picture-gallery. She had gone in.
At the end of the long row of portraits, she had seen
two leaning against the wall, and on examining them
had seen that they were those of the late Graf Arthur
and of her husband. They had come from Paris on
the previous day, but had not been hung up, because

they had been forgotten in the hurry and confusion caused by the preparations for the marriage.

She had then lifted the portrait of Graf Arthur in her arms. It was very heavy, but she had not felt it. She had carried it to her room, and laid it on a table in the middle of the room, and had arranged the wax-candles round it in such a way as thoroughly to illuminate it.

Then with difficulty controlling her nervous horror, she had sat down in the window and waited. The thoughts that had assailed her during those hours of passive endurance were maddening. It was not until the gray of the early morning that she had heard Graf Adam's step. . . .

She had risen to meet him, pale and determined, and as he entered she had seen from his face that he had been drinking deeply.

His eyes had at once fallen on the portrait of his victim.

In the pale gray of the morning, and with the flickering light of the candles falling upon it, the pictured face had seemed alive and about to start out of its frame.

She remembered how Graf Adam had started back on seeing it, and how his drunken senses had reeled with ghostly terror. . . . That was what she had counted upon. . . . She had then said in a clear hard voice: "Begone ! . . . You are a murderer! . . . Your victim stands between you and me. . . ."

And Graf Adam had turned and staggered from the room.

When he had gone, she had sunk back in her chair, with a beating heart and trembling limbs.

A minute later she had heard a shot.

Gräfin Jadwiga closed her eyes, hoping thus to change the current of her thoughts. She clasped her hands over her face. In vain ! The memories of the past persistently haunted her ! . . .

She thought of the wretched time she had passed through immediately after her husband's death—when she had been expected to weep and show grief for his death, although her only feeling had been a dumb horror. She had gone abroad as soon as she could. Life at the castle would have been unendurable in those days.

She remembered how she had shone as a queen of fashion in luxurious Paris *salons*. She had seemed happy then, for her smile had been frequent, and her conversation both brilliant and witty. But in reality she had not been happy, because she had not been able to forget, and because the gay world and its amusements had not filled the void in her heart.

Then temptation had come to her. . . .

A fair-haired, pale, foolish ruler : the curse of his country ; the worthy son of a half-imbecile father and a vicious mother.

Pah! She had thrust him from her presence in disgust.

But hundreds of others had been at her feet, not only rich and handsome, but also good and true-hearted men. And she had loved none of them.

Her hour had at last struck. She had gone to Baden-Baden. . . .

There she had met Doctor Friedrich Reimann, private physician of Prince Sugatscheff, and she had learned to love him as he loved her.

And then she had lost him—by her own fault, as her heart had told her many a time. . . .

She had never been able to make reparation, for he had disappeared immediately after that fatal hour, and though she had tried to find him, she had never been able to do so.

And she had smiled, jested, and ruled over her intimates as before. But her heart was no longer empty, it was filled with a bitter repentance.

She had borne it for a long time, but at last the life she was leading had become utterly distasteful to her.

She had then returned home, in the hope of forgetting what had happened, or, at any rate, of finding relief in no longer being obliged to wear a mask of happiness.

There she had found the man for whom she had sought. She had found him under circumstances she could not understand. But what did that matter? No one could prevent her marrying whom she would. . . .

She longed to repair the wrong she had once done. She longed to be happy, and to make her lover happy. . . .

For the first time in the long hours in which she had been sitting alone in the summer-house she smiled, and it was a smile of hope and love. . . .

.   .   .   .

A breath of spring penetrated even the dark labyrinth of the Jewish town on that day, making the anxious forget their anxieties, and the sick their sufferings. The bright warm sunshine spread hope and joy around. Bocher David found nearly all of his patients better and more cheerful. He talked longer than usual with each of them, and promised almost solemnly to see them next day.

After that he went to the castle. The fat porter told him that the Frau Gräfin was waiting for him in the summer-house in the park. He went there, and entered with his usual expression of gentle gravity.

She hastened to meet him, and putting her hand in his, said :

"Thank you, Friedrich ! Thank you for coming. I have looked forward to this day, and have hoped so much from it. All will be well now."

She paused, as though expecting him to speak.

"I have come, Frau Gräfin," he answered, gravely and quietly, "because you entreated me to do so. And, as circumstances have brought us together again so strangely, I owe you an explanation regarding my dress and my former life. You have a right to it. . . ."

Her eyes filled with tears when she heard him speak so coldly and gravely.

"No, no, Friedrich," she exclaimed ; "you are cruel. You are angry with me, and you have just cause for anger. But I have suffered so terribly ever since the day when I wrote that dreadful letter. . . . Forgive me for the sake of my sorrow and repentance! Oh, forgive me, and don't look at me so sternly!"

"I forgave you long ago," he said, more gently. "I told you so before. But you want to do what is impossible. You want to waken the dead, and to strike moments out of our life that are imperishable, because they are too deeply engraved on our memories ever to be forgotten. I know and can understand how you have suffered," he continued, his voice trembling, "because I can compare your feelings with my own. And now, that you may be spared more pain, and may not form hopes that can never be fulfilled, I entreat you to listen to me, although you asked me to come here to listen to you. . . ."

When he began to speak she had raised her clasped hands in mute appeal to his compassion, but now she let them fall listlessly to her side, and sighed deeply.

She then resumed her seat, and motioned to him to take a chair opposite. He sat down, and went on firmly and decidedly :

"I was born at Barnow, and am the son of the late rabbi. The people there were very kind to me in their own way after my father's death, but I was ungrateful, and mistook their meaning. I left the place after my mother died. I can still remember the dismal, misty autumn morning when I ran away as distinctly as if it were yesterday. I had no money, but Jews are always kind and charitable to the poor. I traveled through Galicia and Poland, remaining sometimes for a few weeks with a rabbi, who was good enough to take me as a pupil; but none of the teaching I received entirely satisfied me. I went on farther. In course of time I reached Wilna, where Rabbi Naphtali, the celebrated Cabalist, has a school. Under his guidance I learned to know the 'Cabala'—that strange, deep, mysterious book, containing the profoundest wisdom and religious teaching of our people. I threw myself into its study with the utmost enthusiasm. That was my misfortune, if you like to call it so. I went through that time of doubt when all dogmatic religion appears to be glaringly false—a time which no young man who thinks at all about these subjects can fail to pass through, and during which he boldly and determinately endeavors to grasp the inconceivable.

"My knowledge appeared small and narrow. I

strove to make it both wider and higher. The German people, with their great poets and thinkers, were irresistibly attractive to me. I studied their language carefully; and by dint of teaching, and exercising an economy that was almost miserly, I at last succeeded in making enough money to go to Germany. I set out at a most fortunate moment for myself, for it chanced that I made the acquaintance of old Prince Sugatscheff at a small town on the borders of Lithuania. He was of the truest nobility: he was a noble-minded man. Prince Alexius, whom you met at Baden-Baden, was his son, Frau Gräfin."

"I remember," she answered, in a low voice.

"Well," he continued, "the young Polish Jew, who knew Lessing, and delighted in Schiller's poetry, awakened his sympathy. He gave me the means of studying. The ancient world was now revealed to me in the books to which I had access at college. I saw it in all its cheerful light-heartedness, and also in its thoughtfulness and depth. But that was not the kind of knowledge for which I thirsted. I then made natural science my principal study. My researches were all confined to the realm of matter. At length the need of leading a practically active life grew more and more apparent to me. The fire of youth had begun to smolder; I gave up trying to raise the veil of Isis, and endeavoring to discover the reason of every natural phenomenon. I became

13

a doctor, and I can now say that I made a reputation for skill in my profession. I had changed my name. David Blum would have 'had many stumbling-blocks and disagreeables in his path that Friedrich Reimann was spared. I did not change my religion with my name—from habit, if you like—for I was indifferent to every form of dogmatic religion.

My practice increased, and I became one of the first physicians in the northern seaport town where I had settled. Then old Prince Sugatscheff was taken ill in Paris, and sent for me. It was his last illness. Before his death, he entreated me to be a faithful friend to his young son, and to accompany him everywhere as his private physician until I thought him capable of taking care of himself, and of withstanding the temptations of the great world. I gave him the promise that destroyed my own career; but he was the only man who had felt a real friendship for me, and he was the only one whom I loved next to my mother.

"I discovered the whole responsibility and painfulness of my position very soon after his death. Prince Alexius was a light-minded and depraved, if not absolutely bad man. I did my duty without caring whether it made him dislike me or not; he respected me at least. It was a time of great anxiety and trouble; one thing alone sustained me, and that was the consciousness of having done my duty. Then we went to Baden-Baden, where I made your acquaint-ance, Frau Gräfin. . . ."

She had until now listened to him with bent head, but at these words she fixed her eyes upon his face, as though awaiting a sentence of life or death. And he continued, with a slight quiver in his voice :

"I will not attempt to recall the events of that happy time to your memory. I loved you with all my heart and soul, and I know that you loved me. If it is any comfort to you to know it, let me tell you that I never doubted your love for me, even at the moment when you wounded me most deeply. But there is one thing I ought to tell you, and that is why I did not then inform you of all that you now know. I did not conceal it from any false shame about my past or my religion, but simply because I never thought of it. You were my first love, and my sad restless heart found rest and happiness in you. I shall always be grateful to you for that short time of unalloyed happiness. First love knows nothing of the past, and does not look forward to the future. The German poet was right when he wrote, 'First love does not know that it must die, as a child does not know what death is, although it may often hear of it.' My love was so great that I did not guess that your love might change when you learned that a Jewish mother had borne me, and that I had been a poor Talmudist. It was not because you were the Gräfin Jadwiga Bor-

tynska that I loved you, but because you were you—
a noble high-minded woman, whose heart beat in re-
sponse to mine. I could never have felt a different
kind of love than this, for the experience of life had
made me grave and proud. What separates us now,
and must separate us for ever, is that you were not
what I thought you, that you could not rise above
the prejudices of your station—it is that, and that
alone. . . .

"I did not just come to this conviction," he went
on, his voice once more sounding clear and full, "during the long years that have passed since we parted ;
I felt it even in that dark hour when I read the letter
in which you wrote, 'If you are really a Jew, if
rumor tells the truth about your past life, all is over
between us now and for ever.' Even then I knew that
the breach was irreparable, and that our love was a
blunder ; so I did not do as another in my position
might have done, I did not try to appeal to what little
love for me might still remain in your heart—I went
away.

"I went away to France, to England, and from
there to America. But I carried my sorrow with
me wherever I went. I suffered much, and had a
hard struggle before I could think of all that had
happened with less pain ; for you had been the
sunshine and spring of my life ; and when my
faith in you was destroyed, it seemed as if faith

in everything else must go with it. But in time
I conquered that feeling. When my suffering was
worst to bear, I devoted my life to the care of the
sick and wretched; for it had changed me. In
the old days I had worked for name and fame, and
from an intense love of knowledge. Pride and self-
seeking had induced me to put out all my powers
to get on in the world, but my own sorrow taught
me to feel for others, and to determine that henceforth my life should be spent in strengthening and
upholding my brother men, as far as in me lay.
I was tired, dreadfully tired, when the battle was
over. I can not bend under the blast of misfortune,
but am broken by it. It is my nature; I can not
help it. Where could I work better than at home?
So I came back to Barnow, to the people who had
been kind to me in my childhood, and to the graves
of my parents. . . . I returned to a faith in
a God of love and mercy, and worship Him in the
religious forms I have been accustomed to since
my infancy. It was not repentance that brought
this about, for I had not been a sinner. It was not
any desire to propitiate the Deity, for I feel neither
hope nor desire of any kind. It was an unspeakably deep, an unspeakably anxious longing for a
firm support to which I could cling in the darkness, sorrow, and confusion in which I was plunged.
. . . I learned to love my people again—my poor,

despised, persecuted people—and, in order to be one with them, I resumed their dress. I have not made a name for myself, as was once my ambition, but have become a poor and simple tender of the sick; but many people down there in Barnow, both Jew and Christian, have turned their hearts to God for my sake. Perhaps I might have gained the fame for which I used to thirst, if I had remained in the rush of life; but here it is better—I do my work and feel no pain. I have ceased to ask, as I often did in the bitterness of anger and misery, why all this should have come upon me, and what I had done to deserve it. I am now at peace, and am therefore happy: I have learned renunciation! . . ."

He was silent. The setting sun cast its light over the lake and the blossoming trees outside, and it also rested like a glory on the calm pale face of the speaker.

After a short pause he continued:

"I did not know that you were the possessor of my native town until you arrived at the castle a few weeks ago. I hoped that we should never meet again: for your sake. I knew that if we did, your pain and repentance would be reawakened; for you loved me too, though it was with a different love."

He ceased speaking. She did not answer. She only sobbed—a low, shuddering sob, as from a broken heart. He rose to go. Then she once more approached him, her face deadly pale, and heavy tears falling from her widely opened eyes.

"So this is the end," she murmured almost inaudibly. "The end. . . . I have found you only to lose you for ever. Friedrich! Friedrich! . . . it will kill me. . . ."

He looked at her compassionately, and then said very gently :

"You will also gain calmness and peace, and then you will be happier. You will then understand that I could not have acted otherwise."

She sighed deeply.

"I am severely punished," she said, with trembling lips. "I must pay for the weakness of a moment with the misery of a long, long life. But there is one thing I can not have you do. You must not despise me. I was induced to write you that letter by the devilish machination of a wretch, who knew how to make use of the prejudice that my people feel against yours—a prejudice I learned in my earliest childhood."

"I thought so," he interrupted her, mildly. "I have felt the effects of that prejudice sorely. I forgive you all the more easily. But who was it?"

"Prince Alexius Sugatscheff," she answered.

"What! That man!" he exclaimed contemptuously; but immediately forced back the words he would have uttered, and continued quietly :

"Thank you for telling me this. It makes it easier for me to forgive myself for having partly broken my promise to the old prince. . . ."

It had grown darker in the summer-house now, and the sun had set.

"Good-by, Jadwiga," he said, in a low voice. "Be happy!"—he took her hand in his—"and never forget that we shall meet again one day."

She could not speak. She stood in the middle of the room listening, until the last echo of his footsteps died away, and then fell fainting on the floor. . . .

The next day found Baron Starsky as troubled in mind and as thoughtful as on the previous day. Gräfin Jadwiga had gone away very early in the morning. Nobody knew where. He was much put out, for in spite of the curious scene he had witnessed between her and "that beast of a Jew," he would perhaps—have married her.

The man against whom his wrath was roused was however at that very moment lovingly stroking the boyish head of the writer of these pages, and comforting him in his sorrow. He had just told the boy that he could be his teacher no longer, for he must now give every moment of his time to the sick and miserable.

.   .   .   .

The Jewish burial-ground at Barnow is a pretty and quiet place—a place that brings thoughts of peace and not of terror—especially in summer, when the blue sky smiles down upon the little field with its fresh green grass and sweet-scented flowers. A blossoming elder-bush is to be found close to the crumbling headstone of every grave.

There is one on the Bocher's grave, as on all of the others. I have often sat under it and thought of the man who sleeps beneath its shadow. And whenever I went there I used to read the beautiful and touchingly simple words upon the headstone, which tell how he had devoted himself to the help of the helpless and the care of the sick, and how he had, like a true hero, died at his post. . . .

He went "home" a year after the interview I have described between him and Gräfin Jadwiga. Low fever was very prevalent in the "Gasse" that winter. David saved all he could, and never spared himself in any way. At last he also took it. He recovered from the fever, but his strength was so much weakened by it, that he fell into a decline, and faded slowly but visibly. He never ceased his labors until he was actually confined to bed. There he lay quietly, and hardly liked people to put themselves out of the way by nursing him.

He sent for me a few days before his death, so I went to see him. He looked pale and ill, and was lying beside the open window, through which the first breath of spring was penetrating his close room.

"I am glad that you have come," he said, with a kind smile. "I have something to say to you before I die. . . ."

He paused a moment, and then went on:

"I was very wrong when I spoke to you about vengeance and retribution for the humiliation we have suffered. I entreat you to forget that, and always wait and think, in the spirit of the words I then quoted to you—'Forgive them, for they know not what they do.' I know that a hasty word is often deeply engraved on a child's mind, so I want you to put your hand in mine, and promise that you will do this, and will try not to allow yourself to think such thoughts as those I uttered in my anger."

I promised him with passionate tears. Boy as I was, I could not help feeling the greatness of soul shown by this man, who, even when he was dying, had time to think of doing good to others.

"You are crying, foolish child," he said, gently. "You should not do so. Have I not often been face to face with death before? And, believe me, death is not terrible—he comes as a friend and comforter to man. It is true that I should have liked to have lived a little longer, and to have gone on with the work I had undertaken; but God, who rules our lives, has willed that it should not be so. His will be done! . . ."

He pushed my hair back from my forehead, and placing his hand on my head in blessing, added:

"Good-by, my child! good-by! and . . . may you be happier than your teacher!"

The last words were said so low that I could scarcely hear them.

One beautiful bright spring morning his attendant found him dead, with a smile upon his lips.

Gräfin Jadwiga is still alive, and is still a beautiful woman. Who can tell whether she is happy, or whether, at the bottom of her heart, there is not a sad remembrance of the man whom she had really loved after her own fashion?

She painted the picture of Christ—that strange product of religious enthusiasm and human love—in Switzerland during the summer that succeeded David Blum's death. The art she had once followed as an amusement now, perhaps, brought her comfort; and the picture also showed that she had understood the nobility and greatness of the self-sacrifice made by the Jew for her sake and his own.

This is the story of the picture of Christ at Barnow. It is strange and sad, as I said before; but do not blame me for that, for my heart bleeds when I remember this over-true tale, which must be regarded as one of the dark riddles of life, and as the doing of that eternal, inscrutable Power that deals out darkness or light, happiness or misery, to the weak human heart. . . .

NAMELESS GRAVES.

(1873.)

NAMELESS GRAVES.

THE last time that I went there was on a beautiful, still autumn day. The sunshine was brightening
the landscape, and the only sound to be heard was the
faint crackling of the withered leaves on the bushes
by the wayside. I followed the winding path that
ran through the fields and gardens. I was alone,
but I knew the place so well that I did not need to
ask my way; for I always go there when I revisit
my old home, and every year I become more attached
to it. Every year the number of acquaintances to
whom it leads me grows more numerous; indeed, the
day will soon come when none of them will be found
in the little town, for all will be there. . . .

It was the "good place" to which I was going;
and as this is the only place to which neither the
Pole's whip nor the covetous hand of the wonder-
working rabbi can reach, the name is a good one.
Here each poor soul is freed from the double ban—
and who can count its victims?—that ground him

down, and stifled the good that was in him. He is
delivered alike from outward humiliation and from
the dark night of ignorance. None of these people
could have been called really happy until they died.
Then, it is true, they know nothing about it, but they
feel that it must be so even while they are alive;
so they have given their burial-ground the beautiful
name of the "good place," and take care to make it
as fair to look upon as they can. It never occurs to
the Eastern Jews to plant trees or sow annuals there;
but the fresh green grass is allowed to cover the
graves, and blossoming elders grow by every headstone. Their burial-ground was the only bit of land
these people were allowed to possess until a few
years ago! . . .

The "good place" at Barnow is as sweet a spot
as is to be found anywhere. I have already described
what it was like in late spring when the elders were
in blossom, filling the air with a perfume that was
almost too powerful, and when the red and purple
berries were beginning to show among the leaves.
In autumn the bushes are shorn of much of their
former beauty, but they are pleasant to look at even
then in their own way. The air in September is so
wonderfully clear and bright, and the autumnal tints
are so vivid, that they lend the somewhat uninterest-
ing landscape a beauty of their own. The moor is
never a cheerful place, and it looks more calm and

solemn than ever in autumn ; but not *triste*—the heather glows with too deep a red, and the foliage of the limes fades into too soft a yellow for that. Here and there a pond may be seen with its dark, clear waters. Any one going to the burial-ground through country such as this, can not fail, I think, to be impressed with its quiet beauty. But perhaps I am not a good judge of that ; perhaps one must have been born in a moorland country to be able to appreciate it. . . .

The " good place " lies on a hill, from which one has an extensive view on all sides. From thence one can see ten ponds, hard by which some villages are situated, whose houses, roofed with brown thatch, resemble collections of bee-hives ; and finally, at the foot of the hill is the town, which has a very respectable appearance from there, although, in reality, it is neither more nor less than a wretchedly dirty hole. One is able to breathe more freely when enjoying such an extensive view, such a wide horizon-line. For to east, north, and south the only limit is the sky, and on gray days the same is the case to the west. But when the air is clear and bright, one can see what looks like a curiously-shaped blue-gray bank of cloud on the western horizon. On seeing it for the first time one is inclined to believe that a storm is brewing there. But the cloud neither increases nor decreases in size, and though its out-

line may seem to shift now and then, it stands
fast for ever—it is the Carpathian range of mountains. . . .

But it is beautiful close to where one is standing
also. It is true that the queer, twisted branches of the
elders are now leafless and bare of blossom and fruit,
but they are interlaced with a delicate network of
spiders' webs that tremble and glow with prismatic
colors in the sunlight. Their deep-red leaves cover
the graves, and between the hillocks are flowering asters. The graves are well cared for ; the Jewish people have a great reverence for the majesty of Death.

To the Jews, Death is a mighty and somewhat
stern ruler, who is kindly disposed to poor humanity,
and draws them to him in mercy. These people do
not like to die, but death is easier and pleasanter to
them than to others, for their belief in immortality
is more absolute than that of any other nation.
This belief is not merely founded on self-love, but
on love to God. Is not God all-just ? and where
would be His justice if He did not requite them in
the other world for all the misery heaped upon them
while they lived on earth ? And yet they cling to
this earth, and regard all the blessedness of heaven as
a state of transition, a preparation and foretaste of
the fuller blessedness of earth after the coming of
the Messiah. It is therefore serving God to bury
the dead. It is therefore serving God to tend the

graves of those who are gone. Even the oldest and
most weather-beaten gravestone is propped up and
steadied by some great-grandson, or perhaps one who
was no blood relation of the deceased, and who was
only moved to do it because the sleeper had once been
a man like himself who had felt the joys and sorrows
of humanity. He was a Jew, and he should find
his resting-place in order when the trumpet should
sound. Some people may look upon this belief as
ludicrous, but I could never feel it so. . . .

One's heart and mind are full of many thoughts
as one wanders up the hill between the rows of graves.
I do not mean those eternal questions which one generation inherits as a legacy of torment from those that
have preceded it, and to which only fools suppose they
can give an adequate answer. Verily, we all hope
for such an answer, for we are all fools, poor fools,
with an eternal bandage covering our eyes, and an
eternal thirst for knowledge filling our spirits. But
why touch unnecessarily on such deep subjects? I
mean questions of a different kind from these. Whoever, for example, walks through that part of the
cemetery where the hill slopes down gently to the
plain below, near the river, can not help thinking of
the evil consequences of two Polish nobles determin-
ing to show themselves humane at the same time.
On four hundred headstones the same year is chiseled
as the date of death—the same year, the same day, the

same hour—it is an unspeakable history. Wet? no! drowned in blood and tears! And it all came from a contemporaneous desire for the exercise of the virtue of humanity! During the time that the Polish kings had power in the land, the Jagellons protected the Jews, who paid them tribute in return. But as the royal authority became of less and less account—still existent, more because it refused to die than because any remnant of power remained to it—the Waywodes, and in the flat land the Starosts, snatched at the chance of taking the Jews under their protection; they were one and all so filled to overflowing with the milk of human kindness. A large and rich Jewish community lived in Barnow, so it was regarded as doing God good service to take care of so great a number of men who were capable of paying considerable taxes with ease. Two Starosts—those of Tulste and of Old Barnow— drew up in battle array, one at each side of the town, and each sent a message to the following effect to the Jewish community : " If you do not choose me as your protector, I shall at once put you and your possessions to fire and sword." The unfortunate Jews had not much time granted them in which to deliberate ; they quickly gathered together all the ready money that they could, and bought the protection of both. This conduct brought down further misfortunes upon the poor people. The Starosts were both philanthropists, and both wished to fulfill the duty they had under-

taken. Neither trusted the other with a work of such
importance, and each determined to put his rival to
the proof; so the Starost of Old Barnow began to
murder and plunder the Jews at one end of the town,
and then waited to see whether the other would do his
duty and protect his *protégés*. But, unfortunately, his
rival was equally determined to try the worth of his
promises, and had been doing exactly the same at the
other end.* Thus neither gained his object. Good
men seldom attain what they strive for! The terrible
carnage lasted for three days and three nights. . . .

The mild autumn sunshine falls as softly on the
graves of these murdered people as elsewhere, and the
asters are larger and more perfect between these
closely massed hillocks; the grasshoppers chirp mer-
rily in the grass and moss that cover them, and the
autumn threads spun by the busy spider wave to and
fro in the gentle breeze. Peace and quiet reign here
also—a peace as restful as in any other part of the
"good place;" and yet it seems to me as though a
sudden cry must arise from these graves, as though
a piercing, agonized cry must break the stillness of all
around; and that cry would not be one of mourning,
but of accusation, and not alone of the Starosts of
Tulste and Old Barnow. . . .

There are many other graves besides these that
bear the same date . . . . those, for instance, that
were filled in the days when a Czartoryski hunted

the Jews because there was so little game left in the neighborhood. And then, again, in this very century, in those three terrible summers when the wrath of God—the cholera—raged throughout the great plain. Grass makes more resistance against the scythe than these people did, in their narrow pestiferous streets, against the great plague. The graves are innumerable, and the field in which they lie is a very large one; but the community now living in Barnow is much smaller than one would think on seeing the cemetery. But the very poorest creature who is given a resting-place and headstone there, has it in perpetuity; none will disturb his rest until, as they say, the last trumpet sounds. . . .

The headstone on every grave is of the same shape. No eccentric monumental tablets are to be seen, and no artistically carved figure is represented on any of the gravestones—the Jewish faith forbids all such adornments. The only difference in these stones lies in the fact that those of the poor are small, and those of the rich large; that the inscription on the poor man's headstone shows him to have been an honest man, and that on the rich man's makes him out to have been the noblest man who ever lived — that is all; for even the arrangement of the inscription is strictly ordained in the Talmodim. The insignia of the tribe is put first, then the name of the deceased, followed by those of his parents, and after that his

occupation in life. Sometimes this last is passed over
in silence, for "usurer" or "informer" would not look
well upon a tomb, to say nothing of worse things. In
such cases the friends content themselves with putting,
"He was indefatigable in the study of his religion, and
loved his children"—and, as a rule, this was true.

Whoever reads these inscriptions will see that he
need go no further in search of the island of the
blessed, or of the garden of Eden, where angels walk
about in human form—that is to say, if he believes
the inscriptions. The Semitic race goes further in
showing reverence for the dead than any other. The
Romans contented themselves with "*De mortuis nil
nisi bonum.*" They demanded that the dead should
be spoken of with kindness and respect, maintaining
that such conduct was only seemly in face of the
majesty of death and the helplessness of the dead.
The Semites go further than this: they exact that
only good should be spoken of the dead. And if any
man is so terrible a sinner that no good is to be found
in him, they keep silence regarding him. . . .

They keep silence. The worst anathema known
to this people is, "His name shall be blotted out."
And so in such cases they do not inscribe his name
upon his headstone. There is many a nameless
grave in Podolian burial-grounds. This is meant as
a punishment, as a requital of the evil the man had
done while on earth.

And, again, it is meant in mercy: for on the day
when the kingdom of God shall come, the heavenly
trumpets can not alone waken the sleepers; the angel
of eternal life is to do that. He will go from stone
to stone, and call the dead by the name inscribed on
the headstone—the righteous to unspeakable blessedness, and the wicked to unspeakable punishment. If
no name is carved upon the stone, he will perhaps
pass on without arousing the sleeper. Perhaps!—all
hope that it may be so, in mercy to the sinner! . . .

There are many nameless graves in the "good
place" at Barnow, and in some cases the punishment
may have been well deserved. It is often the hardest
that has reached the criminal. The black deed has
been done, and the darkness of the Ghetto hid the
crime. The Podolian Jews fear the world, and a
Christian is supreme in the imperial court of justice.
They do not like to deliver their sinful brother into
the hands of an alien. They punish him themselves
as they best can: he must spend much money on good
objects, or make a pilgrimage to Jerusalem, or fast
every second day for years. His crime is hidden as
long as he lives, and it is only after his death that it
is discovered.

Some very curious things are also looked upon as
crimes, and punished in the same way. Whoever
hears of such can hardly help asking a very bitter
question—a very ancient and grimly bitter question,

that can never die out as long as the human race
continues to exist on the face of the earth. . . .

For example, an old beggar once formed part of
the Jewish community at Barnow — a discharged soldier who had been crippled in the wars. No one
did anything for him. The Christians would not
help him because he was a Jew, and the Jews would
not do it because he had eaten Christian food for so
long, and because he was in the habit of swearing
most blasphemously. Perhaps neither of these sins
was entirely his own fault : for no army in the world
has ever put its commissariat under the charge of a
rabbi since the Maccabees fell asleep ; and as for pro-
fane swearing, it may be as much part and parcel of
an old soldier as an acorn is of an oak. But, however
that may be, his co-religionists took both of these
circumstances in very bad part, and provided him
with nothing but daily lumps of black bread, and on
Friday afternoons with seven kreutzers. Even an
old beggar could not live properly in Barnow on so
small an allowance, and the poor old man suffered
frequently from the pangs of hunger. So when the
Day of Atonement came round again—the strictest
fast-day in the whole year—he found no pleasure in
abstaining from food, for hunger was no unusual feeling with him. He was discovered on that day behind a pillar of the bridge with a bit of sausage in
his hand. He was not ill-treated, nor was his allow-

14

ance diminished: and yet fate would have been
kind to him had he died in that hour: for were I
to relate all that happened to the old man, I think
that the hardest heart could not fail to be touched.
But fate is seldom kind: he lived for many years.
When he died, his rich relations put a headstone on
his grave, but left it blank. But I think—I think,
that the dead soldier is not nearly so much pained
by this, as he was by much that they did to him
when he was alive. . . .

Close to the old soldier sleeps a man who met
with a like fate. A very strange man he was—
Chaim Lippener by name, and by trade a shoemaker.
People who follow that trade have often a great liking for philosophical speculation, perhaps because of
the sedentary life they lead. Our Chaim was also a
philosopher after his own fashion. He never rose
above the basis of all investigation—doubt; and his
favorite expression was, "Who knows the truth?"
As the pale little man felt himself unable to answer
the question by means of speculation, he determined
to try whether experience could not help him. He
went from one sect to the other—from the "Chassidim," or enthusiasts, to the "Misnagdim," who were
zealous for the Scriptures; then he joined the former
again, and afterward went over to the "Karaits."
Then he took refuge under the banner of the wonder-
working rabbi of Sadagóra, after which he remained

among the "Aschkenasim"—those are in favor of
German culture—for a year, and finally became a
Cabalist. This he was for a long time; and as his
boots and shoes were good and well-made, people
troubled themselves very little about his midnight
studies and his profoundly mystical talk. But one
cold, white moonlight night, when some men who
had remained until an unusually late hour at the
wine-shop were returning home, they found a man
kneeling motionlessly in the snow at the foot of the
great crucifix at the Dominican monastery, his arms
stretched out as though to embrace the Christ. They
stood still and gazed at the unwonted sight in astonishment, but their surprise was changed into horror
when they saw that the solitary worshiper was none
other than Chaim. They drew nearer, but he did
not hear their footsteps. Suddenly he began to speak
aloud, and in a sobbing, tremulous voice uttered a
prayer in the holy language: it was the blessing
which is prescribed to the traveler when he sees the
sun rise as he journeys along. The listeners were at
once filled with pious wrath; they threw themselves
upon the little man, beat him unmercifully, and
chased him home. Next morning there was great
excitement in the "Gasse;" even the most indifferent
went up to the synagogue to pray, partly from religious motives, to entreat God not to avenge the sin
of the individual upon the community—and partly

from curiosity, for every one wanted to know what penance the rabbi and the council would impose upon the sinner. The congregation did not disperse as usual after the conclusion of the service. The council took their plans. But the culprit was not there, for the excitement and the beating he had undergone had proved too much for his feeble strength— he had fallen ill. As his presence was necessary, some men were sent to fetch him. They brought him on a mattress. A great clamor arose as he was borne up the aisle, and all those who stood near relieved their hearts by spitting upon him. Then the rabbi commanded silence, and began a long speech, in which the place where eternal darkness and eternal cold reign, the place to which the wicked are relegated after death, took a prominent part. Having thus spoken, he turned to the accused and asked him what he had to say in his own favor. But whether it was that the sick man could not speak, or that he had nothing to say, none can tell— he remained silent, and only shook his head. This conduct increased the general indignation ; the rabbi made a solemn remonstrance, and the others spat upon the offender. At length the little man raised himself upon his pillows, looked at the zealots with quiet earnestness, and began to speak. The words he uttered were few, and consisted merely of his favorite question, "Who knows the truth?" The scene that followed may easily be imagined. Those men who were not carried away by fanatical zeal, protected Chaim with their own bodies: had they not done so, his offense had been washed out in his blood then and there. At last, quiet being restored, the rabbi was able to pronounce judgment. I do not remember what the fine imposed on Chaim Lippener amounted to; but so much I know, that he had to leave wife and child, and set out on a pilgrimage to Jerusalem, from whence he was never to return. He was commanded to tell every community he passed on the way what he had done, and to request them to kick him and spit upon him.

He was never able to set out on his pilgrimage, for he fell into a decline, and faded away like snow before the sun. He prayed so much during the last months of his illness, that every one was convinced that he was converted, and had turned from the error of his ways. I am the only person who knew better; and as it can no longer injure Chaim to tell the truth, I will now do so.

When I came home for the holidays in July, his wife came and asked me to go and see him, but begged that it might be in the evening, that no one might notice it. I did so. The sick man was very weak, but he had an immense folio volume resting on his knees, in which he was reading eagerly. After making long and rather confused excuses for the trouble he had given me, he said that he wanted to know whether it was true that the Christians had Holy Scriptures as well as the Jews. When I told him that they had, he begged me to try and get him the book. This request affected me curiously, almost painfully; but it was the wish of a dying man, and—"Who knows the truth?" I found some difficulty in fulfilling my promise, for Chaim could only read Hebrew. I sent to Vienna for a translation the English Bible Society had made for mission purposes in Palestine. The book was a fortnight in coming, and when it arrived I could not give it to the man; but it did not matter, for he probably knew more then, than he could have learned from that book and all the books in the world. . . .

Ah yes! these were strange, very strange, crimes. On that autumn day, as I stood beside the two graves, I felt inclined to stoop down and say to the dead: "Forgive your poor brothers; do not be angry with them, for they know not what they do!" . . .

What a peculiar history the Jews have had! Their strong religion, founded on a rock, was once a protection to them, and saved them from the axes and clubs of their enemies. They would have been destroyed without that protection, for the blows aimed at them were heavy and hard to parry; and for that very reason, they clung to it the more tenaciously, until at last, instead of enlightening their hearts, they made of it a bandage for their eyes. They were not so much to be pitied for this long ago, for then all the world went about with their eyes bandaged. But now, when the light of day is shining in the West, and the dawn has at last broken in the East, they have not raised the bandage one inch. I do not want them to do it too quickly, nor do I want them to throw away their faith ; I only desire that they should open their eyes to the light which is shining more and more around them. . . .

It must be so ; and it will be so. Necessity is the only divinity in which one can believe without doubting or despairing.

Light will come to them ; but no one can tell how long the light will last, or count the victims it will destroy.

It is only by accident one hears of them. The living are silent, and the graves are silent, especially those that are nameless. The history of those nameless graves may be shown by a mark of interrogation, hard but not impossible to decipher.

My curiosity was excited by the last of those blank headstones set up in the cemetery at Barnow. I found it the last time I went there on the beautiful September afternoon I have before described.

It was a solitary grave standing apart from the rest. It lay in the hollow near the river, and close to the broken hedge. This in itself was strange, for the

dead are generally buried next to each other as their
turn comes to die.   A family seldom has a plot of
ground set apart for itself—very seldom ; for all who
sleep here are members of the same family.

An exception had been made with regard to this
grave.   Not another headstone was to be seen far and
wide ; but to the right and left of it, as close to it as
possible, were two other graves—small graves, un-
marked by aught save the tiny hillocks they made.
So small were they, that one could scarcely see them
under their covering of juniper-bushes and red heather.

It was easy to guess who slept there : little boys
who had died before they were eight days old, before
they had been given a name ; and she who lay between them must have been their mother, for the
headstone was that of a woman—one could tell that
from its shape.

Hitherto men alone had been given nameless
graves, because they alone commit crimes, whether
real or imaginary.   The Jewish woman is good and
pious.   It was the first woman's grave I had ever seen
with a blank headstone.

What had she done ?

I puzzled long in the calm sunny stillness of that
autumn day.   I made up one story after another, each
more extraordinary than the preceding one, to account
for it ; but again I was to learn that truth is often
stranger than fiction.

As I sat thinking on the grave, looking from me, and hardly seeing the rainbow tints that the clouds of dancing insects took in the clear air whenever a ray of sunshine touched their wings, I suddenly heard the monotonous drawling sound of mournful voices, and looking up, saw two old men advancing toward me along the hedgerow.

They were busied in the exercise of a pious rite . that I had not seen for so long, that, now that I saw it again, it struck me as it would have struck a stranger. Each of the men was carrying a short yellow wooden stick in his right hand, and round each of the sticks a thread was wound closely and thickly, uniting them to each other ; for one end of the thread was wound round one stick, and the other end was wound round the other stick. Whenever the men stood still, they held the two sticks close together, and sang their strange duet in mournful unison. Then one of them ceased singing, held his stick perpendicularly, and stood as though rooted to the spot ; while the other walked on slowly and gravely by the side of the hedge, singing in high nasal tones, and unwinding the thread as he went, in such a manner as to keep it straight and tight. After having gone about thirty paces, he stood still and silent. The other, meanwhile, began to advance toward him, singing in his turn, and winding up the thread, so that the ball on the one stick grew larger and larger, while that on the other stick grew smaller. Thus there were alternately one duet and two solos.

This is called "measuring the boundaries;" and although it is only done after this fashion in some of the Podolian cemeteries, it is yet done in some way or other wherever the Jews are to be found. On the anniversary of the day on which a near and dear relation has deceased, it is the custom to measure the borders of the burial-ground in which he rests with a thread, that is afterward used for some pious purpose, such as to form the wick of candles offered in sacrifice, or to sew a prayer-mantle. The custom is the outcome of a sad gloomy symbolism, but it would take up too much room were I to attempt to explain it.

I watched the men for a time, and then went up to them, and asked whose was the grave that had interested me.

They looked at me mistrustfully.

"Why do you ask?" one of them at length answered, with hesitation.

"Because I want to know."

"And why do you want to know?"

A direct answer would have been too long, so I made him an indirect and shorter reply.

One of the two worthy but extremely dirty old men—so dirty that one looked at them in wonder—had a very red nose—a circumstance from which one might infer that he was subject to constant thirst, and was of a cheerful disposition. It is always easy to make one's self understood by a person of that kind.

I looked at the man smilingly, as though he were an old friend, and at the same time put my hand in my pocket. . . . "Well—who is it?" I asked.

He watched my movements with visible interest, but did not give way as yet.

"Isn't the name engraved upon the stone?" he inquired.

"I should not have asked you what it was if it had been there."

"Why isn't it there?"

My hand came out of my pocket, but the old man was not yet gained over.

"Why?" he repeated; "because it is a sin even to think of the name of her who lies there! Why should I sin by telling you what it is? why should you sin by listening to it? why should Reb Nathan here sin by listening to us both?"

"Money spent on the poor will wash out the sin," I replied calmly, pressing something into the old man's hand.

But the venerable gentleman was evidently very particular about any matter that might affect the salvation of his soul, so he counted the silver I had given him in a whisper, as if to make sure that I had given him enough. His face now expressed satisfaction; but Reb Nathan, in his turn, began to feel uneasy. He might easily have gone away, and so escaped the sin of listening; but instead of that, he chose another course of action, although he had not a red nose.

When these preliminaries were all settled, the first said, "Whose grave is that?" and the other answered, "Lea Rendar's." Which, being interpreted, means, "Lea, the daughter of the innkeeper, lies there." But I still looked inquiringly at the two men.

"Every one knew her!" they exclaimed, in astonishment. "Lea of the yellow Karezma (inn); the wife of Long Ruben, who lives near the town-hall; Lea with the long hair."

I knew now whom they meant, and my curiosity was turned into an anxious interest.

"What! she was a sinner?" I cried, in amazement.

"Was she a sinner?" exclaimed Reb Abraham, the red-nosed man. "Could there have been a greater than she? No: there never was a greater! She trod the law under her feet! And who will be damned for it? She and her husband—Ruben of the town-hall! For had he not permitted it, the transgression had never been perpetrated."

"Another person will also be damned for her sin,"

cried Reb Nathan—"Gawriel Rendar, her father;
for if he had brought her up differently, she would
never have committed such a trespass against the
law."

"Ah, yes, of course," assented Abraham. Then,
seized with a sudden revulsion of feeling, he pitied
the man in whose house his nose had gained its rosy
hue, and added more gently: "Perhaps the Almighty
may forgive Gawriel after all. How could the poor
father ever have guessed that she would do such a
horrible thing? None of Jewish birth could ever
have thought it! But as for Ruben—that's different;
he is certainly condemned!"

"Was the crime really so terrible?"

"Terrible, did you say?—most abominable!
Didn't you hear of it? An extraordinary story!—a
most remarkable and unheard-of story!"

They then told me this "remarkable and unheard-
of story." And truly it deserved the adjectives they
applied to it, although in a different sense from that
in which they used them.

I can hardly describe my feelings as I write down
what I then heard. In the first place, the whole
affair sounds so incredible. Only those few people in
the West who have a slight knowledge of this ignorant
fanatical Eastern Judaism, will be able to comprehend
that such things can really be. All others will shake
their heads. I can only say that it is a true story;

I did not invent it : it really took place. Besides that, the story is a very sad one. It fills one with sorrow when one thinks of it. . . .

Lea was a very lovely girl. She did not inherit her beauty from either of her parents ; for her mother was a dumpy, little red-faced woman, and Gawriel Rendar, landlord of the large yellow inn on the way to Old Barnow, was an awkward giant with a muddy complexion, and a face much pitted with small-pox. The two sons, who hung about the house, were by no means ornamental members of society. In short, they were a rascally-looking lot, and their chief occupation was to provide bad spirits for the thirsty, and fling those who had imbibed too much of the villainous compound they sold out-of-doors in a rough-and-ready manner. It was in this house and among these people that the loveliest, merriest child grew up into a gentle modest girl. Lea Bergheimer was more like a sunbeam than any one I ever knew.

Her head was crowned with a wealth of shining golden hair. A Jewess is seldom fair ; and when she happens to be so, is, as a general rule, anything but good-looking. The beautiful women of this race have either brown or black hair. But Lea was an exception. Indeed, she was not at all of the Jewish type except in her slender, upright, graceful figure.

Her face was of the highest Germanic type : small, delicate features, rosy cheeks, and deep violet eyes.

The expression of her face was bright and intelligent. There is a seventeenth-century picture in one of the side rooms of the Belvedere at Vienna of a Viennese burgher maiden painted by an Italian. The original was a German girl, but the artist has given her face the impress of the "spirit, fire, and dew" that animate so many Southern natures. That picture might have been a portrait of Lea, the resemblance to her was so strong.

The darkest place may be lighted by a sunbeam; so pretty Lea brought light and joy into the noisy inn. It is scarcely necessary to say how devoted her parents and brothers were to her, and how in their awkward way they delighted to do her honor, watching over her and anticipating her slightest wish in the most touching way. Old Gawriel was well-to-do in the world, for his spirit-shop stood in a central place, and no landlord in Podolia understood better than he the art of watering schnapps, and of doubling the chalked score of any one who went upon tick. But he spent so much upon Lea, that it was really wonderful that he was able to lay by anything. He did not have the girl educated—she learned nothing but what Jewish women in Eastern Europe are taught; but he used to dress her on week-days as rich men did not dress their daughters on New-Year's day.

Her family had unintentionally done their best to

make her vain and coquettish. And other people had
done their part ; the women through their jealousy,
and the men through their admiration. Lea awakened feelings in the hearts of the young men of Barnow such as were seldom to be found there. For, as a
general rule, the long-haired Jewish youth never even
thinks of any girl until his father tells him that he has
chosen a wife for him. He sometimes sees his bride
for the first time at his betrothal, but in a great many
cases he does not see her until his marriage-day ; and
then, whether she pleases him or not, he makes up his
mind to get used to her, and generally succeeds. But
many thought of Lea ; and as she walked down the
street, people would turn and look at her—a thing
hitherto unknown. Even in the "Klaus," where the
quiet, dreamy, and very dirty Talmudists bent over
their heavy folios, her name was sometimes mentioned,
followed by many a deep sigh.

Beautiful Lea knew nothing of this. But other
people took care that she should not remain in doubt
as to whether she pleased them or not. The school-
boys who came home to Barnow for the holidays were
all in love with her and Esterka Regina, another
beautiful Jewish girl whose life was a sad one. Then
there were the young nobles, who were in the habit of
stopping at the door of Gawriel's inn for a glass of
schnapps and a little conversation. But the boldest
of all were the hussar officers, who got into the habit

of-spending hours in the bar-room, without making any way with the girl.

Lea was vain, but she was thoroughly good and modest. Jewish women are, as a rule, kind, charitable, and sympathetic with others; but Lea was even more so than the generality—so the poor used to bless her and reverence her. The girl's great weakness was, that she was in love with her own beauty, and especially with that of her splendid hair. When she loosened her heavy plaits, her hair used to infold her like a mantle of cloth-of-gold, descending to her knees—a mantle of which any queen would have been proud. It was this that gained for her her nickname of "Lea with the long hair." . . .

The Jews of Barnow were firmly convinced that Lea would never marry. The women hoped and the men feared that it would be so. She grew up, was seventeen, eighteen, nineteen years old, and yet had never deemed any of her suitors worthy of her hand. Such a thing was unheard of among the Podolian Jews, who usually marry at a very early age. But old Gawriel acted differently from most fathers—he let his daughter decide her own fate.

Lea's answer to all her suitors was a short, resolute "No." And after the day when Josef Purzelbaum was dismissed in like fashion, although he was the son of the richest man in the whole district—and also little Chaim Machmirdas, who was nearly connected

by marriage with the great rabbi of Sadagóra — no
other suitor ventured to come forward. The rejection
of a member of the holy family of Sadagóra filled
every one with amazement, and many looked upon it
as tantamount to blasphemy. But Lea was not to be
moved, and continued to drive the match-makers to
despair. In the end these good people scarcely dared
to set foot in the inn, although there are no quieter
and more considerate men in the world than the
Jewish match-makers in Podolia. But one of them,
Herr Itzig Türkischgelb, used to say: "I am an old
man, but I have not yet given up the hope of living
to see Lea's marriage and the coming of the Messiah.
But, truly, I think the latter will take place first."
Itzig Türkischgelb always liked his joke.

At last Lea's engagement was announced. And
when the name of the fortunate suitor was made
known, the astonishment of all was even greater than
at the fact of the engagement. For Ruben Rosen-
mann—or Ruben of the town-hall, as he was called,
because of the position of his shop—was neither rich
nor of a pious family; and besides that he was a
widower. He was a handsome man, tall and dignified, and of a grave and serious disposition. He was
particular about his dress, and wore his caftan about
a span shorter than any one else. He had spent two
years in a large town called Brody, and had learned to
read, speak, and write High German. Perhaps this

was the reason that he was looked upon as a free-thinker, which he certainly was not, for he followed all the commands, not only of religion, but also of superstition, with a slavish obedience.

When Lea was asked why she had chosen him of all people, her only answer was, "Because I like him." It was an unheard-of reason for a Podolian Jewess to give : so no one believed that it could be the real reason. Many questions were asked of the match-makers, but they could throw no light on the subject. Even Türkischgelb had to confess that this engagement was not brought about by his diplomacy. Ruben had sent him to Lea ; but the girl had refused to listen to him, saying, "Let him come and speak to me himself if he has anything to say."

Ruben went to see her. The two young people had a long conversation that lasted fully two hours. No one, not even the girl's parents, knew what they had talked about during their interview. But old Gawriel heard Ruben say in a loud impressive voice : "Very well—if you have set your heart upon it, I consent. It is not a sin in the sight of God, although our people regard it as such. Keep your secret carefully ; for, were it discovered, it would cause the destruction of us both." The father tried in vain to persuade Lea to tell him her secret.

The marriage took place soon afterward. Lea was lovelier than ever as she stood under the "trauhimmel." And yet her richest ornament, her golden hair, was wanting. No married woman is allowed to wear her own hair, which is always cut short, and sometimes even shaved, before the wedding. The head is then covered with a high erection made of wool or silk, called a *scheitel*. Stern and ancient custom demands this. For a married woman to wear her own hair, would not merely be regarded as im-modest, but as a terrible sin against God. Lea per-mitted no one to lay a finger on her hair, but lock-ing herself into her room, cut it off with her own hands. . . .

Contrary to expectation, the marriage was a happy one ; and more wonderful still, Lea was a humble, obedient wife. The most envious could not deny that Ruben was a lucky fellow. No one knew it better than he did, and, when he heard that Lea hoped soon to be a mother, his joy knew no bounds. But, unfortunately, this hope was not fulfilled ; the child was born dead, and before it was expected. The doctor said it was in consequence of a chill from which Lea had been suffering ; but the rabbi of Barnow was of a different opinion. He sent for Lea, and asked if she had not broken some commandment in secret, and so brought down upon herself the judg-ment of God. Lea turned very pale, but answered firmly, " No, rabbi."

This happened in spring. One autumn day, a

year and a half afterward, Lea had a son; but it
only lived six days. The doctor said it had died of
apoplexy, like many other new-born babies. Lea
wept bitterly; but when the rabbi came to her and
repeated the question he had before asked her, she
again answered shortly and firmly, "No, rabbi."

In the following summer Lea knew that she was
to become a mother for the third time. She felt
oppressed by a foreboding that the same sorrow as
before would come to her. She took every precau-
tion, and Ruben watched over her anxiously and
tenderly. But when the Day of Atonement came
round, she insisted on spending the whole day in the
synagogue fasting, in spite of her husband's remonstrances and the doctor's having forbidden her to do
so.

That was the cause of her destruction.

The old synagogue was dreadfully close that day,
and worse than close; it was filled with a most disagreeable and sickening odor of candles, and of an
uncleanly congregation that had spent hours within
its walls praying and weeping. It was an atmosphere
in which the strongest person might have been overcome with faintness; so that its effects on a delicate
woman in Lea's condition may be readily imagined.
Her head began to swim, and, uttering a low cry, she
fell from her prayer-stool in a swoon.

The women quickly surrounded her, and tried to

bring her to herself. They loosened her dress, and thrust two or three smelling-bottles under her nose at the same time.

All at once they started back: a wild shriek from a hundred throats echoed through the building; it was followed by silence—the silence of dread. . . .

Lea's *scheitel* had become displaced, and her glorious hair, which had been confined within the *scheitel,* flowed over her shoulders, and crowned her pale beautiful face as with a golden halo.

That was Lea's secret.

The scene that followed can not be described; an idea of it can hardly be conveyed to a stranger. The stillness was broken by wild shouts of rage, curses, and struggling. Quick as lightning the news flew to the body of the synagogue, where the men were praying; and its effect was the same there as in the women's part. At first horror and astonishment produced an intense stillness; then the men seemed filled with an insane fury, and rushed into the women's "school." Had Lea just confessed that she had murdered her children—and the Jews regarded infanticide as the worst of crimes, as even more wicked than parricide—their wrath could not have been greater. But in the eyes of these ignorant, superstitious people, Lea's hair had borne silent witness that she was indeed guilty ! . . .

It was the holiest day in the year, and she against

whom their wrath was raised was a weak woman, and was, moreover, in a condition that ought to have pleaded for her with the most savage of men. But who knows how far pious zeal might not have led these fanatics? It had often before carried them to incredible lengths. Ruben forced his way through the ranks of infuriated men, his anger and pain giving him strength to do so. He lifted his wife like a child, and, supporting her with his left arm, pushed a way for himself and her through the crowd by a vigorous use of his right arm. He then rushed down-stairs, and home through the streets, pursued by the curses of his co-religionists. The October wind blew his wife's hair sharply in his pale face as he ran, and almost blinded him.

Lea soon recovered from her faint; but when she looked round and saw her hair hanging about her like a cloud, she shrieked out, and fell into violent convulsions. The doctor hastened to her; but he only succeeded in saving the life of the mother, not that of the child. Next morning the Jews of Barnow told each other that the judgment of God had fallen upon the sinner for the third time.

Ruben was as though petrified with grief. And when he was summoned before the rabbi in council that very morning, he obeyed the mandate as calmly as if he had not been the culprit to be tried. He returned no answer to the curses that were heaped

upon him, and, when put upon his defense, gave
short and bold replies to the questions addressed to
him. He was asked whether he had known of his
wife's sin. Yes, he said, he had. Why had he suffered her to commit such a wickedness? Because it
was not wicked in his eyes. Did he recognize what
had now befallen him as a judgment of God? No;
because he believed in an all-wise, all-merciful God.
Would he at least consent to cut off his wife's hair
now? No, for that would be breaking the promise
he had made her when they were engaged. Did he
know the punishment he was bringing upon himself
by continuing in his sin? He did, and would know
how to bear it.

This punishment was the "great *cherem*," or excommunication—the worst punishment that the community could inflict upon one of its members. Whoever is thus excluded from the congregation is out-
lawed by them, and it is regarded as a good deed to
do him as much harm as possible, both socially and
in his business relations. Neither he nor anything
that belonged to him might be touched except in
enmity; his presence could only be permitted with
the object of doing him an injury. *Cherem* loosens
the holiest ties, and what in other cases would be
a terrible sin is, under such circumstances, regarded
as a sacred duty—the wife may forsake her husband, the son may raise his hand against his father.

It is a war of all against one—a merciless war, in which all means of attack are admissible. No love, no friendship, can venture to break down the barrier of excommunication, contempt, and loathing that incloses the culprit. It is a fate too awful to contemplate, a punishment terrible enough to break the most iron will. He who falls under this ban, generally hastens to make his peace with the rabbi on any terms, however humiliating.

Ruben thought this too high a price to pay, although he felt the curse of the excommunication doubly, both in his person and his work. No customers came to his shop. But he did not give way. He turned for protection to those who were bound to help him, and appealed to the imperial court of justice in Barnow. It is a punishable offense in Austria to use the *cherem* as a means of extortion; and, in the best case, when there is real and just cause for the infliction of punishment on an offender, it is nothing but an audacious attempt of a community to arrogate to itself the functions of the state. The sympathy of Herr Julko von Negrusz, district judge of Barnow, was aroused by Ruben's tale, and he did what he could to help him; but naturally he could not do much. He summoned the rabbi before his court, and punished every injury or indignity that was put upon Ruben which could be proved against any one in particular. But in most cases

15

the mischief was done in the dead of night, and the prosecution of the rabbi only served to increase the fanatical rage of the people. As for the shop, Herr von Negrusz had no power to force any one to buy their sugar and coffee from Ruben if they did not wish to do so.

The war of parties lasted all winter, and well into the spring. In April the rabbi was sentenced to six weeks' imprisonment. When he was set free, the community showed their joy by illuminating the streets and breaking Ruben's windows; otherwise, nothing was changed—Ruben remained firm. He was growing visibly poorer. His father-in-law continually entreated him to give way, but in vain. More than that, Lea, who had wept away all her youth and beauty during that terrible winter, and who, now that the spring was come, knew that she was again to become a mother, entreated her husband to allow her to cut off her hair. Perhaps the poor woman had been so influenced by the superstition of her neighbors, that she had really begun to think that it might cause the death of her child were she to continue to wear it. But Ruben shook his head sternly, and answered—"No; keep your hair; and if there is a God, He will not desert us—He will give me the victory."

In most cases it is a dangerous thing to place one's belief in the existence of God on the answer to a question such as this. It was so here : Ruben was conquered. What remains to be told I will relate in as few words as possible. . . .

In the following November another son was born to Lea. The child was a strong, healthy little fellow, and the mother's heart was at rest about him. Six days passed ; then the rabbi summoned his most faithful adherents to his presence. " The father is under the ban of *cherem*, and the mother wears her own hair ; but the child is innocent. If we remain idle, the child must die as his brother died, because the mother continues to sin."

This was what the rabbi said—that is to say, it was probably he who spoke ; but the originator of the horrible deed was never discovered. This was the deed of darkness perpetrated by the zealots.

About midnight of the sixth day after the baby's birth, some masked men burst into Ruben's house, overpowered both him and the nurse, dragged Lea out of bed, and cut off her hair.

Two days later Lea died in consequence of the fright she had had. The child, which had taken a fit soon after the men had broken into the house, died a few hours before its mother.

Ruben remained at Barnow until the judicial examination was over, although he hoped but little from it ; for when the Jews are determined to be silent, no power on earth can make them speak.

Then he went away. Many years have passed away since then. He, probably, has also found rest, and sleeps away the dark sorrows of his life in some other corner of the world.

I have already described Lea's grave, and there is nothing more to be said.

I must add a few words in conclusion, that come from the bottom of my heart:

Forgive them, be not angry with them, for they know not what they do!

THE END.

Milton Keynes UK
Ingram Content Group UK Ltd.
UKHW021959241123
433237UK00004B/129